'Understanding the present depends on [illegible] history – and history does not have a single reading. This is a timely, prescient and informative book that helps Western observers to look through an Eastern Orthodox lens at current crises.'
Nick Baines, Bishop of Leeds, England, and author of *Freedom is Coming*

'A timely book on a crucially important subject for today.'
Averil Cameron FRHistS, FBA, Former Professor of Late Antique and Byzantine History, University of Oxford, and author of *Byzantine Christianity: A Very Brief History*

'Katherine Kelaidis offers a brilliant exposé of the transformation of the Russian Orthodox Church into Putin's propaganda machine, highlighting the historical roots and fundamental ideas that have led the Church to justify Russia's invasion of Ukraine.'
Sergei Chapnin, Senior Fellow at the Orthodox Christian Studies Center, Fordham University, New York City

'An easy-to-read and insightful book on a difficult and disturbing conflict. Kelaidis brings into sharp focus otherwise disparate and often bifurcated dimensions of a complex subject overly simplified in the West.'
John Chryssavgis, theological advisor to the Ecumenical Patriarch and author of *Light Through Darkness*

'Russia's aggression against Ukraine has many dimensions, including a religious one. The Orthodox Church is being used by the Kremlin and its propaganda machine to justify the war, making it not merely acceptable but even desirable to the average Russian. The war in Ukraine marks a major crisis in the global Orthodox community. Katherine Kelaidis addresses this crisis in a comprehensive way, exposing the many ways in

which the Russian Church is not only supporting the war but also projecting Russia's power elsewhere in the world. There will be other books addressing these issues, but this one is to be welcomed as an early, informed and incisive response to the war and the crises it has caused.'
Cyril Hovorun, Professor of Ecclesiology, International Relations and Ecumenism, Sankt Ignatios Foundation, Stockholm, Sweden

'Kelaidis argues persuasively that Russia's war against Ukraine has religious and moral underpinnings with dangerous implications far beyond its borders. She writes evocatively and engagingly to explain the twisted interpretations of history that are motivating both Vladimir Putin and his ecclesiastical accomplice, Patriarch Kirill. The war has shaken the Orthodox Christian world into recognizing that this "ugliness is the product of the same heritage that has also produced so much beauty". But the war is not just an "Eastern European problem". Kelaidis traces the powerful alliance of Westerners who are sympathetic to the underlying Russian religious and moral motivations that seek to undermine liberal democracy worldwide.'
John A. Jillions, Visiting Professor of Religion and Culture, the Institute for Orthodox Christian Studies, Cambridge, England, and former Chancellor, the Orthodox Church in America

'A valuable guide to the religious dimensions of the war between Russia and Ukraine – past and present – beautifully delivered in a brisk and lively prose that is bound to engage and inform both specialists and the general public.'
Alexander Kitroeff, Professor Emeritus of History at Haverford College and author of *Greek Orthodoxy in America*

‘A must-read for everyone concerned about the most chilling aspect of Russia’s aggression against the Ukrainian people: the religious one.’
Sister Vassa Larin, host of the popular online programme, *Coffee with Sister Vassa*

‘The role of religion in the war in Ukraine is clearly a hugely important dimension of the story, but it has received relatively little attention in our press coverage and political debate; this treatment is an original, and in some areas unexpected, way of shedding light on this critical subject.’
Edward Stourton, journalist and presenter of BBC Radio 4’s *The World at One*

Katherine Kelaidis is a writer and historian. She holds a BA in Classical Languages from the University of California at Berkeley and a PhD in Classics from Royal Holloway College, University of London.

She is the Director of Research and Content at the National Hellenic Museum in Chicago, and an associate fellow of the Institute of Orthodox Christian Studies, Cambridge, England.

A senior correspondent for *Religion Dispatches*, she also serves on the editorial board of *The Wheel*, an independent journal of Orthodox Christian thought. Her current work focuses on contemporary Orthodox Christian identity in geopolitics and the role of historical memory.

HOLY RUSSIA? HOLY WAR?

Why the Russian Church is backing Putin against Ukraine

Katherine Kelaidis

spck

First published in Great Britain in 2023

Society for Promoting Christian Knowledge
The Record Hall, 16–16A Baldwins Gardens
London EC1N 7RJ
www.spck.org.uk

British Library Cataloguing-in-Publication Data
A catalogue record for this book is available from the British Library

ISBN 978–0–281–08972–7
eBook ISBN 978–0–281–8974–1

1 3 5 7 9 10 8 6 4 2

Typeset by Westchester Publishing Services
First printed in Great Britain by Clays

eBook by Westchester Publishing Services

Contents

Part 3
THIS IS NOT JUST A PROBLEM FOR UKRAINE

Preface

The vast majority of the material contained here was written between 2018 and 2022 for *Religion Dispatches* (a publication of Public Research Associates), beginning around the time that the Ecumenical Patriarch of Constantinople created the independent Orthodox Church of Ukraine (a rival to the Moscow-tied Ukrainian Orthodox Church) through to the full-scale Russian invasion of Ukraine and the first year of that conflict. The few pieces that pre-date 2018 largely provide context for later events. These pieces have been arranged chronologically within three broad themes (Parts Two, Three and Four, below), so the date of first publication is provided at the top of each. Some pieces have been lightly edited in view of subsequent events or merely for consistency of style and format.

Part One provides a brief history from the time of Constantine the Great (circa 330 CE) to the present from the perspective of the Christian East. Any historical account endeavouring to cover such a large passage of time (approximately 1,700 years) is inevitably not comprehensive and some events and figures have been omitted.

Prologue

On a cold afternoon in the October of 1993, on a primary school playground outside Denver, Colorado, I learned that some people (or maybe even most people) think that Vlad Dracula is a villain – even a monster. This came as an enormous shock.

Late October is strange at the foot of the Rocky Mountains. The aspen trees, which had turned the mountain sides and creek beds, not to mention city sidewalks and highway medians, blazing shades of yellow and orange just weeks before, suddenly drop their leaves, transforming them from glimmering torches to stick piles. Most days the sun still shines in a giant, pale-blue sky, even though the temperature has rapidly reached freezing. By the time spooky costumes are selected and plastic skeletons propped up on suburban lawns, at least one snowstorm has covered everything with mounds of white powder. In Colorado we send children out to play, even when it is snowy and freezing. And standing on the playground – the only place you could stand without getting covered in snow – one afternoon just three days before Halloween, Bob Watson told me he would attend our cafeteria-based Fall Fest (which everyone knew was a Halloween Party) as Dracula himself. When Bob said the name I froze; my eight-year-old brain making the connection that a lifetime of vampire films had failed to inspire. Did Bob think that Vlad Dracula was . . . a monster? This was my first indication that perhaps Bob and I had been learning very different versions of history. And that this might really matter.

I grew up in the tight-knit Greek diaspora community of the American Intermountain West in the 1990s. The Orthodox

Church was at the centre of my life, and the life of my family and community. Byzantine-style icons covered the walls of our houses. Ancient cycles of fasting and feasting determined the food on our dinner tables. We prayed in the loping syllables of Byzantine Greek, while lighting candles and burning incense. In Church School on Sunday afternoon and Greek School on Wednesday night, I learned about the Fall of Constantinople and the dark days of Ottoman rule. I memorized the names of heroes who resisted, names like Vlad Dracula, Voivode of Wallachia, who bravely confronted the Turkish armies and died fighting them. My evangelical classmates (like Bob) carefully portioned out part of their allowance each week to be sent to various missionary efforts to Christianize Russia, newly liberated from seven decades of Communist rule. However, I knew that Saints Cyril and Methodius had taken care of baptizing the Slavic people a thousand years earlier and that the godless Soviets were a mere blip in a millennium-long story of a Christian nation. For some reason, I did not wonder why Bob had never heard of the two Byzantine monks. And when NATO bombs fell on Serbian soldiers a few years later, I heard my beloved grandfather – a man deeply proud of being both an American and a Democrat – rail against a Clinton administration that seemed entirely ignorant of everything that had been suffered by the Serbs at the hands of Bosnia's Ottoman ancestors. My grandfather's father had been born on the island of Crete in 1889, while Crete was still part of the Ottoman Empire, and was ten years old when the Cretan Revolt forced the Ottomans from Crete once and for all. Decades later, when my postgraduate work brought me into contact with cornerstone texts of Postcolonial Theory, I began to understand the forces at work in my grandfather's mind on those nights when we sat watching the news from Belgrade and Sarajevo. At the time, however, I did not ask why the newsreader did not mention the events that haunted my grandfather's mind.

I noticed and did not notice (in the strange way that children both question and accept their world) that we never talked about the Byzantine Empire or the Ottomans at my 'American' school, just as you would never know that the Hundred Years War ever happened should the only history you learned be the sort taught in church basement classrooms on Sunday afternoon and Wednesday nights. There was, for me, only a momentary discomfort the first time a teacher painted a picture of the Crusaders that was sympathetic or declared that the Roman Empire 'fell' in 476. Just as there were two Easters and two Christmases, just as you spoke Greek at home and English at school, I believed it was only natural that there were two versions of history, two entirely different stories about the past, each suited for one of the two worlds in which I grew up.

For most people in the West, even those with a more cosmopolitan outlook, these worlds have been largely kept apart in the 30 years that separate my childhood memories from the world of today. Vampires, Rasputin, perhaps the carnival at a Greek church or a copy of a Byzantine-style icon propped up in the corner of a room have been their only points of contact with the Eastern Orthodox world. For most – even for the objectively small, but relatively large, numbers of Western converts who have journeyed into the Christian East in the past four decades – the 'other half' of the Christian world remains a combination of the mysterious and the obscure.

However, increasingly, this ignorance is no longer an option. Every war fought on the European continent since 1945 has been in some way related to Orthodoxy and its unique understanding of history: the Turkish invasion of Cyprus, the Balkan Wars and now the shocking Russian invasion of Ukraine, all involve one or more traditionally Orthodox Christian nations and have their roots in the peculiar view of the past that belongs to the Christian East. Twenty years ago, shocked North Americans and Western Europeans discovered that many Muslims were still angry about events long forgotten in the West; apparently, they had not yet learned that the Western narrative of history is not a universal one. The Orthodox Christian world has its own story about how we got here and why. It is a story that Westerners must learn if they want to understand the present.

Part 1

SHADOWS OF THE PAST

The New Rome

The Roman Empire did not fall until 29 May 1453. If this date seems to be off by a thousand years, it may be because you have been taught to conflate the Western half of the Roman Empire with the whole Empire and that you call the Greek-speaking Eastern half of that Empire 'the Byzantine Empire'. That such a place existed would have come as a great surprise to those who lived there – most of whom, even after an Ottoman Sultan led Muslim prayers in the Hagia Sophia, the great cathedral of the East, continued to call themselves 'Romanoi' – Romans.

It is in the fracturing of the Roman Empire between the Latin West and Greek East (a division which, truth be told, predates Christianity as the imperial religion) that the two halves of the Christian world began to divide, succumbing to the same cultural, economic and political tensions as the rest of the Empire.

In 330 CE, the Roman Emperor Constantine the Great moved his capital from Rome to Byzantium, an ancient Greek city perched on the edge of the Bosporus. He rebaptized the metropolis *Constantinople* (the city of Constantine – a lack of modesty was a requirement for an emperor). Constantine's decision reflected what was an increasingly apparent reality: the cultural, financial and administrative heart of the Roman Empire was no longer in Italy but in the Greek-speaking Eastern Mediterranean. It was also an effort to create a Christian stronghold in the eastern half of the Empire, where the old religion and culture had remained significantly entrenched. The emperor aimed to use Christianity as a means of unifying his sprawling, diverse, contentious and increasingly frayed domain. The thought that the most economically and culturally powerful part of that realm would remain outside of the faith was simply unacceptable.

Almost immediately, moving the capital drastically increased the power and prestige of Constantinople's local bishop. The city had previously been under the authority of the Metropolitan of Heraclea, but throughout the fourth century, with the Emperor nearby, the Bishop of Constantinople's position grew in influence; it was after all in his cathedral that the Emperor worshiped each Sunday. The Council of Constantinople in 381 CE, convened by Emperor Theodosius, declared the See of Constantinople second in order of precedence among all Christian bishops, behind only the See of Rome.

The Council of Constantinople had been called by Theodosius as a matter of theological and political urgency. When he came to the throne in 379, Theodosius I inherited an empire in crisis (that is to say, even more crisis than the nearly perpetual crisis of the previous two centuries). In the East, following the death of Constantine, a succession of sympathetic emperors had allowed Arianism, a prevalent heresy which held that Christ was in fact not divine, to blossom. Constantinople in particular had become an important Arian centre. For Theodosius, who accepted the divinity of Christ as explicated by the Nicaean Creed, the presence of Arians in the capital, not to mention any number of the most powerful posts in the state and church (including as Bishop of Constantinople), was not only theologically untenable, it was also politically dangerous. After all, Christianity had been elevated to the imperial faith in no small part to provide unity. Intensifying discord with theological squabbles was not acceptable.

Not that things were any better in the Latin West. Goths and other Germanic tribes, long outside of Roman control, were streaming into imperial lands. In the Balkans in particular, the Goths were leaving a path of destruction in their wake, largely unchecked by the Roman army. Unable to recruit citizens, the Roman army had increasingly to fill its ranks with very Germanic tribesmen; this created a threat.

Arguably, it was at the Council of Constantinople that the division between the Western and Eastern halves of the Christian world became inevitable. There is little doubt that Arianism, the heresy that Theodosius was so eager to put down, the thing he had identified as the source of the chaos, was concentrated in the East; therefore, he summoned only the Eastern bishops to the imperial city. Once they had arrived, the Nicaean bishops of the East got to work solidifying their power, not just over the Arians but also over the Western Latin-speaking Church. In the end, the Council issued seven canons, or decisions. Only one, the first, was explicitly about Arianism as a dogmatic position. The other six focused on the governance of the Church, including the Third Canon, which read simply: 'The Bishop of Constantinople, however, shall have the prerogative of honour after the Bishop of Rome; because Constantinople is New Rome.' In these 21 words, the power balance within the Christian world was forever drastically altered. Not only would the relatively young Church of Constantinople enjoy a superior status to the Church of Antioch, the Church of Alexandria and the Church of Jerusalem, the oldest Christian sees, but now Constantinople's status as a *New Rome* was not just a matter of political expediency; it was also seen as a theological reality.

It did not take long for the Bishop of Rome, Pope Damasus, to see the danger posed by this canon, issued by a council to which neither he nor any of his bishops had been invited. His response was to call his own council the following year. The Eastern bishops refused to attend, instead sending a letter that reiterated what the Council of Constantinople had decided. While he continued to defend his position as head of the Christian world, the Pope was faced with a stark reality: Rome was isolated from the rest of the Church's power centres geographically, culturally, linguistically and, soon, also politically.

It is here perhaps more than at any other point that the histories of West and East begin to take on their own characters and to this day what exactly happened in Constantinople in 381 remains the subject of debate, ecumenical dialogue, scholarly conferences and Twitter vitriol. What was the Second Ecumenical Council? Was it a meeting of all the Churches whose decisions bound all Christians for all time? Or was it merely a gathering of local bishops, needed to put down a problematic and persistent heresy? Moreover, what did the creation of a New Rome mean for the old one? Western histories tend to ignore Rome's growing isolation, choosing instead to focus on the ways that fracturing secular authority elevated the role of the papacy in its own domain. Likewise, for Eastern Christians, the focus is nearly always on the fact that 'four out of five patriarchates' were in the East, with little attention being paid to the growing political power of Rome in the West. Furthermore, for both Roman Catholic and Eastern Orthodox hierarchies, the claim to legitimacy and universal authority stems from this initial, existential dispute. The lines had been drawn, and things were not going to get better.

Rome never fell

In January of 395, Theodosius died, leaving the Empire to his two sons. The eldest son, Arcadius, became Emperor of the East and the younger son, Honorius, Emperor of the West. While there had been co-emperors before (this had in fact largely been the status quo throughout the fourth century), it was with the death of Theodosius and the division of the Empire between his sons that this split became permanent, at least in the minds of some. It is, for instance, not without cause that Arcadius is often named as the first 'Byzantine' emperor.

Honorius was only ten years old when he became ruler of the West and, in the early years of his reign he relied almost entirely on Stichilo, a general of mixed Roman and Vandal ancestry. Stichilo's influence on his young charge was – he even became his father-in-law (although eventually, Honorius would grow contemptuous of his mentor and have him executed; that, however, is a different story). A skilled military strategist and veteran of Rome's attempts to repel the Germanic threat, Stichilo understood the threat to Rome, which lacked much in the way of natural and manmade defences. Rome might be a suitable capital for an unchallenged superpower, but it was not sufficient for a declining state under constant threat of attack and invasion. Thus, in 408, Honorius transferred the capital of the Western Empire from Rome to Ravenna, a northern Italian city that had first been federated into the Roman Republic in 89 BCE.

The move came not a moment too soon. The Visigoth king Alaric, a former ally of Theodosius, had turned his attention to Italy. On 24 August 410, Alaric and his Visigoth forces entered Rome, sacking the city for three days. It was not a particularly devastating rampage, but this was the first time that Rome had fallen to a foreign army in 800 years and the psychological effect was intense. The Empire's remaining pagans blamed the failure of Christians to acknowledge the old gods, while Christians pointed their fingers at the pagans being allowed to continue their demonic rites within the confines of Christ's earthly kingdom. Such was the tension and confusion that some have suggested that the Roman pontiff at the time, Pope Innocent I, may have hinted at allowing private pagan worship to resume within the boundaries of Rome.

The idea that Pope Innocent might have been 'soft on paganism' has been a particularly useful and enticing idea for many Eastern Christians, because he is also arguably the last Bishop of Rome to act as head of the whole Church and to have been treated as such by the Eastern bishops. For example, it was to Innocent that John Chrysostom, that giant of Eastern Christian theology and liturgy, appealed when he was deposed from his office by a synod overseen by Theophilus of Alexandria. The Pope looked favourably on the golden-mouthed cleric's plea; however, Arcadius was firmly in Theophilus's camp and refused to allow Innocent to convene any gathering that exerted authority over the Eastern Church or to make any decision as to who would serve as bishop in his capital.

While the Western Empire would limp forward for nearly 70 years more, the events of 408 set the stage for what is now regarded as 'the fall of Rome'. A thousand years later, Renaissance thinkers and artists would portray those events as a great and abrupt trauma, although it is hard to say whether the people who lived through them actually saw them as such. For those later commentators, the Barbarian king Odoacer had ousted the infant Western Emperor Romulus Augustus and brought centuries of Roman dominance to a final cataclysmic end. The curtain dropped.

The truth, however, was much more complicated. While he was certainly not a Roman, Odoacer's exact origins are unknown, in no small part because he lived most of his life in the imperial context. He was a Christian, though an Arian one, and by 470 an officer in the ever-dwindling Roman army. By 475 he was the head of the Germanic peoples bound by treaty to Rome, an official Roman office. That same year, Orestes, a Roman aristocrat from the province of Pannonia Savia (which was in the north Balkans) was appointed by the Western Emperor Julius Nepos as *Magister militum* and made a Roman patrician. It was a poor choice of deputy.

Orestes seized control of the government at Ravenna and sent Julius Nepos into exile in Dalmatia, where he would be assassinated five years later. With Julius Nepos out of the way, Orestes elevated his son Romulus, then between 12 and 15 years old, to the rank of Augustus. With the young usurper on the throne, Odoacer and the other Germanic tribesmen in Italy saw an opening by which they might improve their increasingly untenable situation. Odoacer sent a petition to Orestes demanding land and permanent settlement in Italy for the Germans. It was only after he was rebuffed that Odoacer sought another course of action. Gathering the once loyal Germanic tribes together, he marched on Ravenna and captured the city, forcing the young Romulus to abdicate. Not long after the abdication, news arrived that Zeno, the son-in-law of Leo I, had become Emperor of the East. Odoacer and the Roman Senate sent an envoy to Constantinople, carrying with them the imperial insignia and the message: 'The world needs only one ruler.' Zeno, for his part, would appoint Odoacer to be *Magister militum* (although he would later decide this was a bad idea and have Odoacer assassinated). In short, for those alive at the time, the 'fall of Rome' was largely just another shake up in the imperial structure and Odoacer, Rome's alleged 'conqueror', just another Roman functionary who would, it seems, routinely accept imperial honours.

That being said, there is no doubt that the events of 475–476 brought significant changes to the political status quo, although it is worth noting that nothing happened in that year that did not have some immediate parallel in the recent Roman past. For example, it had long become unnoteworthy for a local governor to have Barbarian roots, and efforts to reunite the Empire were nearly as old as its division. It is thus easy to see why, particularly for those in what was then the much more stable and prosperous East, the idea that the Empire had 'fallen' seemed like utter nonsense.

The question as to whether the Roman Empire ceased to exist in 476 is one of those fundamental questions of historical orientation that continue to divide Eastern and Western Christianity. Further, it is discomforting and confusing from the Eastern perspective that, in the early sixteenth century, not long after the Roman Empire really did succumb to the Ottoman invasion, the post fifth-century Roman Empire was renamed in the West by a German scholar the 'Byzantine Empire', thus erasing a thousand years of survival at the stroke of a pen and dismissing the Christian East and its empire from the history of the Western Christian world.

The conversion of the Slavs

Even if you accept that the Roman Empire continued after 476, it is difficult to argue that, from the sixth century onward, and particularly after the death of Justinian I, there was not an increasing power vacuum in the West. Eastern emperors became progressively less able, and then less willing, to rule the largely impoverished, culturally desolate West and various Germanic kings, chiefs and local warlords sought to make themselves Emperor. This rush to claim the imperial throne had many unexpected side effects, not least of which was that it greatly accelerated the conversion of the remaining pagan tribes. Consequently, by the end of the ninth century, non-Christian Europeans were almost exclusively confined to the far north and far east of the continent and the race was on to convert them, especially since the growing division between the Eastern and Western Churches also gave rise to increasing competition for converts as Rome and the Eastern bishops sought to expand both their power and their sphere of influence.

One of the largest and richest un-Christianized kingdoms was that of the Kyivan Rus. Today, the modern states of Russia, Ukraine and Belarus all claim this massive kingdom, founded upon Varangian and Slavic intermingling, as an ancestor. Rising rapidly in power and prestige, by 860 the Kyivan Rus were responsible for a successful raid on Constantinople itself. The raid, and fear of a repeat, offered a powerful motive to bring the Kyivan Rus into the Church and thus (hopefully) into line. Nonetheless, the nineth-century Byzantine efforts to convert the Kyivan Rus were spotty at best and do not seem to have yielded anything like the success emperors and bishops were quick to claim.

For one thing, Byzantine sources were prone to treating the 860 raids as a Byzantine victory, courtesy of the intercessions of the Virgin Mary. This belief, in turn, gave rise to the conviction that the Rus, having been so awed by the miracles they witnessed at Constantinople and so devastated by their defeat, sent envoys to the Patriarch asking him to send a bishop. But this is only one (highly suspect) account, and the truth of when and to what extent Christianity penetrated nineth-century Kyiv and its people remains a subject of some debate.

However, there was a contemporaneous missionary effort among the Slavic people that, broadly speaking, was much more successful (depending on how one judges success). In 862, Prince Rastislav of Great Moravia sent a letter to the Patriarch of Constantinople, Photius and the Emperor, Michael III, asking that they send missionaries to Christianize his subjects. It is clear that Rastislav's motives were political, not religious. He had come to his throne in 846 by way of support from the East Frankish king (and was no doubt baptized, under the authority of the Roman Church, as a condition of that support). However, by the early 850s he was ready to cast off his overlord and by 855 he launched his first full-scale rebellion.

As part of his efforts to rid himself of Louis the German, Rastislav also sought to curtail the activities of Frankish missionaries in his domain. When Rome did not answer his request to send replacements, he turned to Constantinople. The chosen missionaries were two brothers, Cyril and Methodius, from the northern Greek city of Thessaloniki. The brothers enjoyed a significant degree of success, particularly among the Bulgarians, not least because they used the vernacular language of the people to whom had been sent to preach. In a foreshadowing of things to come, Cyril and Methodius, while preaching among the Slavs, encountered other missionaries sent from the

West under the authority of the Pope, who considered the Slavic lands to be rightfully his mission field.

Recognizing the popularity and success of Cyril and Methodius (or perhaps just out of curiosity), Pope Adrian II invited them to Rome, where they were warmly received. The Pope conferred on Methodius the title of Archbishop of Sirmium (present-day Sremska Mitrovica in Serbia) and authorized the use of the Slavonic liturgy in the Slavic lands. However, the brothers were still popular in Constantinople, and it remains unclear which bishop they were actually working for, although today they are commemorated in both the Orthodox Church and by Eastern Catholics as the 'Baptizers of the Slavs'. It is worth noting that this honorific paints a broad brush over the complexities of nineth-century missionary efforts among the Slavic peoples, allowing modern Russians and Ukrainians (for example) to claim Cyril and Methodius as their missionaries. It is an important simplification, one that no doubt colours the view of religious self-perception and adds an additional century to Russian Christianity.

Despite the success and popularity of the brothers, their efforts did not have any long-term impact among the Kyivan Rus. The *Primary Chronicle*, the authoritative history of the Eastern Slavs, notes that, although a substantial portion of the Kyivan Rus did convert to Christianity during the nineth century, it was far from the majority. And, importantly, the Prince of Kyiv remained a pagan. It would be another century before the Kyivan Rus, including their ruling family, could be completely brought within the boundaries of the Christian faith.

Olga of Kyiv was the key that opened that final door. Born sometime around the beginning of the tenth century, Olga was of Viking origin. Little is known of her life before her marriage, while still a teenager, to Prince Igor I of Kyiv. Igor was the son and heir of Rurik, who had founded the ruling Rurik dynasty of the Kyivan Rus. In 943 she had a son with the prince and, two years later, when Igor was killed in battle, Olga assumed the regency for the toddler prince.

The first woman to rule the Kyivan Rus, Olga was a fierce, effective and pragmatic ruler, instituting the first legal reforms recorded in Eastern Europe. It is her political shrewdness that complicates our understanding of Olga's conversion to Christianity, blurring the lines between religious faith, political expediency and personal ambition.

What we do know is that, sometime in the 950s, she travelled to Constantinople to visit the Emperor Constantine VII. It was during this time that she was converted to Christianity, although the sources remain unclear as to whether she was actually baptized in Constantinople or later, after she had returned home. Regardless, Olga's conversion in Constantinople was a serious blow to Latin efforts to bring the Kyivan Rus under their sphere of influence. Of course, this did not mean that the East had yet been entirely successful. Despite Olga's conversion, her son, Sviatoslav, remained a committed pagan his entire life. It was not until the conversion of her grandson, Vladimir, that a proper prince of the Kyivan Rus would enter the waters of baptism.

The myth surrounding the conversion of Vladimir, Grand Prince of Kyiv, has the air of a fairy tale about it, with the *Primary Chronicle* describing a contest of faiths that resembles a kind of bridal pageant:

> Vladimir summoned together his vassals and the city elders, and said to them: 'Behold, the Bolgars came before me urging me to accept their religion [Islam]. Then came the Germans and praised their own faith [Western Christianity]; and after them came the Jews. Finally the [Eastern Orthodox] Greeks appeared, criticizing all other

> faiths but commending their own, and they spoke at length, telling the history of the whole world from its beginning. Their words were artful, and it was wondrous to listen and pleasant to hear them. They preach the existence of another world. "Whoever adopts our religion and then dies shall arise and live forever. But whosoever embraces another faith, shall be consumed with fire in the next world." What is your opinion on this subject, and what do you answer?'

The prince is thus advised by his councillors to visit each of the contenders to observe their faith in action. When he at last comes to Constantinople, and particularly the Great Church of the Hagia Sophia, he is awed by its beauty and remembers his grandmother's conversion amid the same splendour years before. However, Vladimir is not baptized on the spot – at least not according to the *Primary Chronicle*. Instead, he waits a year, until after he has captured the imperial city of Kherson, whereupon he demands the Emperor's sister, Anna, as a wife. The Emperor refuses until Vladimir agrees to be baptized, a request to which Vladimir ultimately acquiesces, gaining the Orthodox faith and an imperial bride all in one very well-timed conquest.

Whatever the actual circumstances of Vladimir's conversion, it was the final nail in the coffin of Slavic paganism and the founding act of Slavic Orthodoxy as it exists today. This has some pretty shocking implications in light of current events, not least of which is that, upon his conversion, Vladimir set about making his capital a major seat of his new faith. It was thus in Kyiv that the first great Slavic cathedrals were built and to Kyiv that the Patriarch of Constantinople sent a metropolitan bishop. In a faith tradition where place and antiquity are equated with legitimacy, this is no small matter. Moscow was quite literally not even on the map in 988, a history that has been inconvenient for many a Russian propagandist ever since.

The Great Schism and the Crusades

The conversion of Vladimir holds many puzzles for historians, in both West and East. As we have seen, it affords a very good case for seeing Kyiv, and not Moscow, as the chief city of Slavic Christianity. At the same time, anyone vaguely familiar with the popular timeline for 'the Great Schism' (that is, the official fracturing of the Roman Catholic and Eastern Orthodox Churches) will note that 988 is 66 years before 1054 (the date normally associated with 'the Great Schism'), and yet it is very clear from the story of Vladimir's conversion that he at least saw the Western and Eastern halves of the Christian world as two distinct faiths. The truth is, as you might have already begun to gather, that the break between the East and West was brewing long before 1054. Moreover, the mutual excommunications of 1054 were not as dramatic or significant at the time as they would later appear in hindsight. In fact, one might argue (as I have) that the final division between East and West was not ultimately complete until the Protestant Reformers made one final bid for union nearly 500 years later. This is all to say that we are talking about a very, very messy divorce.

The slow burn of that divorce erupted into a fire in 1053 when Archbishop Leo of Ohrid (a region in what is today the Republic of Northern Macedonia), no doubt at the behest of Michael Cerularius, the Patriarch of Constantinople, wrote a letter to John, the Bishop of Trani, a seaport on the southern Adriatic coast of Italy. The letter condemned a host of Western practices, including the use of unleavened bread for the Eucharist. Despite the specified addressee, the condemnation was directed at all

Western bishops, including the Bishop of Rome – the Pope himself. This is evidenced by the fact that the letter's dispatch coincided with Michael Cerularius closing all the Latin churches in Constantinople, an act of aggression that could only upset the tense status quo that had emerged during the centuries of growing hostility between East and West.

The reply of Pope Leo IX was either one of two letters: *In terra pax* in September 1053 or the ever so slightly softer *Scripta tuae*, dated January 1054. Both letters were absolutely the wrong response in that both offered strident defences of the prerogatives and privileges of the Roman See. Considering that the notion of papal primacy had become the biggest point of contention from the point of view of the Eastern Churches, being reminded that they must submit to the Pope was not exactly going to calm Michael Cerularius and his deputy. Even the need for co-operation against the Norman intrusion into southern Italy, which threatened both Byzantine land and Papal dioceses, was not enough to bring about reconciliation. On 16 July 1054, Michael Cerularius, as he prepared to celebrate the Divine Liturgy in the Hagia Sophia, was given a papal bull declaring his excommunication. In response, the Patriarch convened a synod four days later to excommunicate the legates who had delivered the proclamation. It is clear from contemporary accounts that most did not consider the excommunications to be of any lasting significance. In fact, 30 years later, when the Emperor Alexios Komenos asked the Holy Synod of Constantinople whether there had been a break with Rome, the Emperor's bishops answered that there had not.

This was, importantly, the answer the Emperor was looking for, because he was also looking for help. For centuries, the Roman Empire had been, largely unsuccessfully, repelling advances from Muslim armies on its eastern flank. The Seljuqs, a Turkic Sunni Muslim empire, had taken most of Asia Minor and were encroaching on the gates of Constantinople. Unable to stop the Seljuq advance, Alexios sent an emissary to Pope Urban II pleading for assistance.

What could have been an occasion of reconciliation marked yet another grave misunderstanding. Alexios had intended merely to collect a small number of mercenaries from among the Latins. Instead, Pope Urban II, recognizing the advantages of ridding Western Europe of some of its excess population and redirecting the aggression of its feudal warlords, not to mention being enticed by the prospect of renewed relevance and influence in the East, journeyed to France, the land of his birth. There, he convened the Council of Clermont at which, on 27 November 1095, in front of a crowd of noblemen and clergy, he preached a passionate sermon calling upon pious Christians to join their brothers in their struggle against the Muslim infidels.

We do not have a definitive version of this sermon; however, whatever he said must have been inspiring indeed, for it unleashed some unexpected consequences of its own. Urban had intended for the first retinue of soldiers, an orderly collection of French nobles and their feudal vassals, to leave on 15 August 1096, the Feast of the Assumption of the Virgin Mary. This, however, was not what happened. Seemingly unbeknown to the Pope, a charismatic preacher known as Peter the Hermit had set about rallying his own army of peasants and low-ranking knights. This ragtag band of untrained, undisciplined would-be soldier-pilgrims set out several months in advance of the planned army, spurred on by a succession of astrological events that they interpreted as a sign of divine blessing.

The results were predictably disastrous. Before even leaving Western Europe, the so-called People's Crusade launched an unprecedented series of pogroms against the Jewish communities of France and Germany. Eight hundred were murdered in Worms and a thousand killed in Mainz. Similar massacres occurred at Cologne, Trier and elsewhere. Condemned by the clergy and the nobility, such pogroms were forbidden in subsequent Crusades. The damage, however, had already been done. It has been estimated that between a quarter and a third of the Jewish population of the Rhineland was killed during the first six months of 1096.

It was in Cologne that Peter the Hermit completely lost control of his makeshift army. He had stopped to preach in the hope of gathering more Crusaders, but his army was unwilling to wait for him or their German brothers. Taking Walter Sans Avoir as their new leader, they continued east, reaching the border of the Eastern Empire at Belgrade. There, they encountered a very surprised Byzantine commander who, without warning or orders, refused them entry into the city, leaving the Crusaders to pillage the countryside for supplies. Eventually, with the countryside stripped bare and the population terrorized, it was decided to allow them to carry on to Nis, where they were allowed provisions while awaiting word from Constantinople.

At Nis, Peter, now reinforced with German recruits, joined up with Walter's forces. There, the Byzantine commander promised them food and an escort to Constantinople if they would just leave, which they did the next morning. On the road to Constantinople, they managed to pick a fight with some locals in which they lost a quarter of their number and were thoroughly routed. Thus, by the time they arrived in Constantinople on 1 August, their reputation had preceded them, and a baffled and possibly frightened Alexios had them quickly ferried across the Bosporus. Not surprisingly, when Peter's men eventually joined battle with the Seljuk army they had been meant to be fighting all along it was a disaster. Peter's army was thoroughly crushed at every turn, so that the Emperor was ultimately forced to send the famed general Constantine Katakalon to save what remained of the People's Crusade.

If the People's Crusade had been the worst of what the Crusades wrought, then perhaps something of the union of Christendom might have been salvaged. However, the Fourth Crusade, nearly 200 years later, proved even more damaging – a horrific series of events which, although largely forgotten in the West, were to leave an indelible mark on Eastern Christian history and identity.

The Second and Third Crusades followed over the next fifty years. When Pope Innocent III came to the Throne of St Peter in January of 1198 and immediately set about making a Fourth Crusade the central mission of his papacy. At first, he was unsuccessful; there were simply not enough spare soldiers. France and England were at war with each other, and the German states were engaged in a struggle against papal power that foreshadowed the Reformation. The Pope's efforts were ultimately saved by Fulk of Neuilly, a priest from Neuilly-sur-Marne, today a suburb of Paris. In 1199, at a tournament organized by the French nobleman Theobald III, Count of Champagne, a grandson of Elanor of Aquitaine and Louis VII, Fulk rose to preach. What the Pope had failed to do, the country preacher accomplished; a crusading army was raised, electing Theobald as their leader.

However, before the newly formed army could set out for Egypt, their stated goal, Theobald died and was replaced at the helm by Boniface of Montferrat. Recognizing that Germany, France and England (the normal source of Crusaders and supplies) would be of little use, he turned to the rising maritime powers in Italy, particularly Genoa and Venice. Genoa was uninterested, but Venice offered to transport 33,000 men to Egypt for the stately sum of 85,000 silver marks. The procurement of Venetian support was fateful.

An Eastern province in Late Antiquity, by the eighth century Venice had elected its own leader with the blessing of the Emperor. By the dawn of the thirteenth century, the city had grown wealthy through a combination of trading (including being the only medieval European city to be actively involved in the slave trade) and crusading. It was the unquestioned regional power and positioned as a serious rival to the power of Constantinople. Consequently, when the Crusaders arrived in Venice without sufficient money to pay for their passage, the Venetians decided they could pay their bill with some light mercenary work, sending the Crusaders off to bully port cities along the Adriatic coast. This arrangement culminated in an attack on the city of Zara (now Zadar in modern day Croatia). The raid on the city was a bloody one, marked by extensive pillaging and outbursts of fighting between the Crusaders and the Venetians as they squabbled over the spoils. When the news of a Crusader attack on a Latin Christian city reached the Pope, a horrified Innocent III immediately sent notice to the rogue army to cease their activity and return to their stated objective of fighting Muslims not Christians or risk excommunication.

It was, however, already too late. The Fourth Crusade was unquestionably now an instrument of Venetian power and its eyes now turned to Constantinople. The rivalry between the two great cities had already turned violent 20 years earlier when Andronikos I Komnenos had waged a bloody pogrom against the Western Christians of Constantinople (most of whom were Venetian or Genoese by origin), an event known as the Massacre of the Latins. The memory of this tragedy was still fresh in the minds of Venetians as the armies of the Fourth Crusade turned toward *Nova Roma*.

On 13 April 1204, the armies of the Fourth Crusade entered Constantinople. For three days they pillaged the city, destroying ancient art, desecrating monasteries and looting churches. Thousands died at the hands of the Crusaders. When word reached the Pope, he was again horrified, rebuking the marauders in the strongest possible terms but the damage was already done. The Sack of Constantinople accomplished what excommunications and theological discord could not; it permanently divided the Church of the Greeks from the Church of Rome, and it instilled in Eastern Christians an almost reflexive distrust of the Christian West that remains to this day.

And yet it is arguable that most Westerners do not even know that the Sack of Constantinople happened. For them, the Crusades are the stuff of Hollywood films and turkey-leg-packed Renaissance festivals, but for their Eastern counterparts, the Crusades are moments of severe and permanent historical trauma. For people in the East the Crusades (and particularly the Fourth Crusade) were an act of betrayal that would set the stage for centuries of misfortune to come, all laid at the feet of supposedly Christian brothers.

Ottoman occupation

The sense of betrayal has only grown over the centuries, in no small part because neither Constantinople, nor the Empire of which it was the capital, ever completely recovered from the 1204 invasion. A collection of so-called 'Crusader States', most importantly what became known as the 'Latin Empire', were set up in and around Constantinople following the city's pillage. This period is tellingly called the *Frankokratia* (the Frankish rule) and lasted for 58 years, until the great city of Constantine was retaken by a Greek army under the command of Alexios Strategopoulos. Finding an unguarded spot in the city walls, Strategopoulos led 800 men into the city, restoring Emperor Michael VIII Palaiologos to the Roman throne.

It was a throne that was less stable than it had ever been. For the next two and a half centuries, the remnant of the once unchallenged Roman Empire limped on, fighting off attacks from the Christian Bulgarian Empire, the Serbian Empire and various Latin kingdoms from the west and the ever-growing Muslim Ottoman Empire from the east. By 1450, all that was left was a few square kilometres surrounding the legendary city.

Mehmed II was only 19 years old when he became the Ottoman Sultan in 1451, following the death of his father. He immediately turned his attention to strengthening the Ottoman navy, with an eye to taking Constantinople once and for all. The Emperor quickly understood what was happening and turned to the West for help, as Alexios Komenons had done centuries before in his struggle against the Seljuks. This time, however, aid from the West would only come in exchange for the promise of submission to the Roman Church. The Emperor

Constantine XI wrote to the Pope, agreeing to do what a succession of prior emperors had failed to do, and impose union. It is unlikely that the Emperor could have made good on this promise, as Constantinople was still rife with anti-papal sentiment, but it was his only hope.

To be fair, the embattled Emperor and his predecessors did try. Between 1431 and 1449 there were significant efforts to heal the rifts of the 1053 excommunications. The Eastern Emperor, John VIII Palaiologos, was keen to obtain the strategic support that ecclesiastical union would bring and entered negotiations with Pope Eugene IV. Even if the terms they reached were not exactly agreeable, they could be lived with, and the Eastern Emperor duly consented to union. On 18 September 1437, Pope Eugene summoned the bishops to Ferrar for a council dedicated to bringing unity to Christendom. The Eastern contingent, more than 700 strong and presided over by the Patriarch of Constantinople, with representatives of the Patriarch of Antioch and the Patriarch of Alexandria in tow, arrived in early April 1439. By the 9th of the month, the assembly was debating the most hotly contested theological differences between East and West. The debates continued for months. With money running low and the threat of plague looming, it was decided to move the assembly to Florence. On 6 July 1439 an agreement, the *Laetentur Caeli,* was adopted by all but one of the assembly; the representative of the Patriarch of Alexandria refused to sign. To make matters worse, a month earlier the Patriarch of Constantinople had died. The Eastern bishops, facing widespread opposition to union back home, both from laity and monastics, felt unable to move forward. The attempt at unity collapsed.

It might not have mattered, however, in terms of imperial military readiness. The Hundred Years War, the Reconquista, and the endless warring of the Holy Roman Empire meant that no Western prince was particularly eager to send support.

Although a few military vessels arrived from the Italian mercantile states, it was never going to be enough to counterbalance the Ottoman threat.

And so it was that, in the early April of 1453, Mehmed began to lay siege to the city and, on 29 May, the Ottomans entered Constantinople.

As was customary in medieval warfare, the Sultan allowed an initial period of looting as a means of rewarding his troops, although many have suggested that Mehmed did take steps to prevent the most extreme forms of pillage; he was interested in ruling the famed city, not destroying it. Besides, most of what was valuable had already been taken or destroyed by the Crusaders in 1204. Nonetheless, the days immediately following the Ottoman entry into Constantinople were disastrous. Churches were pillaged and burned. Thousands of citizens were killed or forced into slavery. Captured girls were stripped naked and displayed in the market, changing hands for a few silver pieces.

By the time the Sultan arrived in the city on 1 June, he found a city half destroyed and half abandoned. Amid the carnage, he made his way to the Hagia Sophia and, like so many visitors before, was awed by the sight of the immense cathedral, which made for an impressive sight, even after having been assaulted for days. It was a Friday and so the Sultan ordered that Jumu'ah prayers be performed in the giant Basilica. The Hagia Sophia was now a mosque.

It is difficult to explain the catastrophe that the Ottoman conquest represented for the people of the Christian East. The Empire was lost. The Hagia Sophia was lost. For nearly five centuries after 1453, the majority of Eastern Christians would live under Muslim rule. While the relative harshness of that rule would vary widely across the centuries, the psychological effect arguably still lingers today. It was from the rubble of the Ottoman conquest that the fundamental modern self-perception of Orthodox Christians began to emerge. For having remained loyal to the True Faith, the Orthodox had been abandoned by the heretical Christian West and conquered by the armies of Muslim infidels. The Orthodox faithful and their beleaguered Church were the Suffering Servant of Isaiah 53:

> He grew up before him like a tender shoot,
>   and like a root out of dry ground.
> He had no beauty or majesty to attract us to him,
>   nothing in his appearance that we should desire
>   him.
> He was despised and rejected by mankind,
>   a man of suffering, and familiar with pain.
> Like one from whom people hide their faces
>   he was despised, and we held him in low esteem.
> Isaiah 53.2–3

This self-perception has been translated in a number of ways. Over kitchen tables and from pulpits, the idea that the suffering endured by the Orthodox faithful for their 'loyalty to the truth' has not only been *their* salvation but that of the *whole world*, has often been repeated. Like much of the hidden mythos of colonized or otherwise marginalized people, the identification of Orthodox Christians with Isaiah's Suffering Servant does not frequently make its way into Western histories, missed by Western scholars not privy to those whispered conversations that form every culture's sense of self. However, it is fundamental to the Orthodox view of the world and a part of Orthodoxy identity the West would be wise to recognize.

There were practical realities to contend with as well. Without an emperor, the Eastern Church's ability to function fundamentally broke down. For example, with no emperor it was unclear who had the authority to call a Church council. Papal authority had grown in the West largely in response to the power vacuum created by the collapse of secular authority, but a thousand years of continued imperial rule had prevented that in the East. In fact, the East had in many ways shaped its self-image around the notion of opposition to papal, or even papal-esque, authority. In practical terms, this was only possible because of the power exerted by the emperor, and the loss of that emperor raised questions about how the Church could continue in his absence. The stage was set for Orthodoxy's principle modern dilemma. Could this imperial Church survive in any meaningful way after empire? One might say that the jury is still out on this point.

The Third Rome

One obvious solution to the dilemma of having to govern an imperial Church without an empire is to obtain a new empire. However, in the fifteenth century, the options for Orthodox Christians on this front were severely limited. Only the Rus nations remained free. Among them the most powerful ruler was the Grand Prince of Moscow, and the opportunity to become the new Emperor was a very attractive one to this upstart prince.

Almost immediately following the fall of Constantinople a now largely lost epic began circulating among the Slavic people, particularly in the Grand Duchy of Moscow. The *Tale on the Taking of Tsargrad* is attributed to a mysterious figure named Nestor Iskander, whose biography and even existence are as much matters of myth as truth. In the text, the author claims to be a Russian, captured as a child by the Ottomans and forced to convert to Islam; however, he says, he remained a Christian in his heart. From the surviving extracts, it is clearly a shockingly good story, offering its main characters, including its chief villain, Mehmed II, a level of psychological depth and complexity that is not common in medieval (or even early modern) texts. Inordinately good character development aside, the poem presents serious problems when it comes to the veracity of the events it describes. For example, contrary to what we learn from Nestor, the Patriarch was not in Constantinople at the time of the conquest; neither was the Empress, for she had already died. However, it was neither its fantastic characters nor its lack of historical accuracy that mattered to the *Tale*'s original audience. That audience was more concerned with a prophecy contained within it. Referencing a Greek legend (for which, tellingly, we have no other source), the *Tale on the Taking of Tsargrad* declared that Constantinople would one day be liberated by a race of blond and fair-skinned people. And Russian readers of the story knew exactly who those people were.

There was a host of non-literary reasons to see the emerging Grand Duchy of Moscow as a likely successor to Constantinople. A shrewd and opportunistic prince had come to the throne, and he saw a way to move beyond being a mere prince of a Slavic backwater and to claim the Roman Empire for himself. He just needed the right bride, a bit of nerve and a lot of luck.

Finding appropriately imperial blood came first. When his first wife, the Russian Maria of Tver, died, Ivan was free to re-enter the marriage market. No longer content with a local girl, he began to look elsewhere for a bride whose lineage and connections would help him fulfil his grand plans. As luck would have it, there was a girl with purple blood in Rome who was also in need of a husband.

Following the Ottoman conquest, substantial numbers of refugees had poured out of the Empire and into Western Europe. Most headed to Italy, where they would help fuel the Renaissance, although some found their way to the Iberian Peninsula, where their expertise as sailors and navigators would contribute to the era's Portuguese and Spanish maritime prowess. Among these refugees was Sophia Palaiologina, the niece of the last Byzantine Emperor. Sophia was raised in the papal courts and had in fact been 'adopted by the Papacy' after the death of her father. While she remained ostensibly Orthodox throughout her time in Italy, her Latin guardians assumed that she was, for all practical purposes, a Catholic, or at least loyal in some way to the men and institutions who had reared and provided for her. When the princess was of marriageable age, Pope Paul II, hoping to bring the Orthodox Russians (if not the whole of the Orthodox Church) under Rome, arranged for her marriage to Grand Prince Ivan III of Moscow and All Rus. His plan was simple: convert the husband through the wife and the nation through the husband. A giant caravan led by a standard bearer carrying the Latin cross was sent to accompany the princess to her new home; however, when the royal train arrived in Moscow, the procession was stopped. The Latin cross was not allowed past the gate and into the city. Sophia became Ivan's imperial and Orthodox bride. Now purple Roman blood flowed through the Muscovite princely house.

But imperial blood was nothing if it did not have a free empire to go with it. For nearly 100 years, the Grand Duchy of Moscow, as well as most Rus states, had been dominated by the Golden Horde, a daughter kingdom of the Mongol Empire, whose leader was known as the Khan and whose people became known as the Tartars. In 1476, Grand Prince Ivan III became the first Russian prince in centuries to refuse to pay tribute to the Khan. In response, Ahmed Khan organized an army and set out for Moscow. The two armies met at the Ugra River, where the Khan was ultimately forced to retreat into the steppe. It was assumed that the Tartars would return to try and extract their tribute, but while preparing for his second attempt to force Ivan to submit, Ahmed was killed in an ambush by a rival Tartar warlord. Ivan III became the first ruler of Moscow to rule independently in nearly 200 years; he also would begin to call himself *tsar*, a Slavic corruption of *caesar*. He and every king of Russia after him would be a ruler in the shadow of the Roman line.

Of course, at its core, the claim to be a 'Third Rome' was not only political but theological. Rome, as it had been understood for more than a millennium within the Christian context, needed not only an emperor but a patriarch, a bishop whose authority, even in the anti-papal Orthodox world, was more than that of some local hierarchy. For the Muscovites, this was a prickly issue, one filled with plenty of inconvenient history. The Grand Duchy of Moscow was a political, cultural and, above all, spiritual successor to the Kyivan Rus. But it was not the only one, and in order to lay claim to the imperial mantle the Muscovite princes had to find a way for their claim to supersede all others. And that was not going to be easy.

From the time of the conversion of Olga and Vladimir, the chief bishop of the Rus had been a metropolitan bishop, under the authority of the Patriarch of Constantinople, with his seat in Kyiv. Throughout the thirteenth and fourteenth centuries, as the Mongols moved rapidly across Rus land, the power and prestige of Kyiv went into sharp decline. It swiftly became a less than ideal location for any cleric looking to exercise authority and influence outside of his diocese. In 1328, a Constantinople-born cleric named Theognostus became Metropolitan of Kyiv and All Rus. He chose Moscow as his permanent residence, eager to be near the contemporary centre of Rus power. While he retained the title 'Metropolitan of Kyiv', neither he nor any of his successors would reside there.

Even after he had moved to Moscow, the Rus's chief bishop remained under the authority of Constantinople, although that meant increasingly little in practical terms. In 1448, the Rus bishops, who had almost universally rejected the Greek efforts toward union with the West at Ferrar and Florence, elected their own leader, Jonas, without seeking either advice or permission from Constantinople.

Jonas's election placed the Moscow-based church into a *de facto* schism with Constantinople. This divide would only widen as events rapidly progressed over the following decades. The fall of Constantinople in 1453 made the already shaky attempt at a union between East and West, undertaken at the Council of Florence, even more unstable. In 1467, Metropolitan Gregory of the Bulgarians, one of the Eastern bishops appointed by papal agreement, in the wake of the Council of Florence, rejected the union with the Roman church and recognized the jurisdiction of Patriarch Dionysius I of Constantinople. In return, Dionysius demanded that the church in the Grand Duchy of Moscow submit to Gregory, a demand to which Moscow refused to submit.

However, time was on the side of the city and her rulers. By the reign of Ivan III's great-grandson, Feodor, the Patriarch of Constantinople had been in Ottoman captivity for nearly 100 years, impoverished and isolated. Feodor, who likely suffered from some intellectual disability, was under the control of a regency headed by his brother-in-law Boris Godunov. Godunov and Moscow's chief bishop, Job, worked together to make the decisive move and formalize Moscow's honoured place within Christendom. Sending an envoy to Constantinople, they offered support and protection in return for the Patriarch giving his blessing for the office that had begun as the Metropolitan of Kyiv to become the Patriarch of Moscow.

After protracted negotiations, inevitably influenced by the fact that the Patriarch of Constantinople found himself essentially captive in Moscow by the time they concluded, the Patriarch offered his assent. Job, a bishop who, like his predecessors over the past century, had not been brought to his throne with any input from the Patriarchate of Constantinople, would receive the dignity of a Patriarch from that same discarded bishop, easily forgotten behind enemy lines. The first Patriarch of Moscow and All Rus took his throne on 5 February 1589. As part of the deal, the Patriarch of Moscow retained the ecclesiastical territory that had once belonged to the Metropolitan of Kyiv. Where once Kyiv ruled Moscow, now Moscow ruled Kyiv.

The decision was far from popular, particularly in what is today Ukraine. After the Patriarch of Constantinople left Moscow, four of the nine bishops in the Ruthenian territories of the Polish–Lithuanian Commonwealth (what is today western

Ukraine) gathered in the city of Brest and signed a declaration of their willingness to unite with Rome, a declaration quickly accepted by the Pope. The Union of Brest, as this arrangement came to be known, was at first wildly successful, enjoying the support of the King of Poland and the Grand Duke of Lithuania. However, it was not long lived, as various Orthodox parishes continually revolted against papal rule. Today, the existence of the Greek Catholic Church (sometimes called the Byzantine Catholic Church) remains the most visible artefact of the Union of Brest.

If you have been watching the news recently, this points to a host of problems. For anyone thoroughly confused by the religious mayhem of modern-day Ukraine, 1589 is a good place to start trying to understand what is going on. It is without a doubt true that the political and religious histories of Kyiv and Moscow, of Ukraine and Russia, are indelibly intertwined; but this does not mean that Ukraine and Russia are indistinguishable and interchangeable. As the Union of Brest demonstrates, there has always been at least some resistance to Moscow asserting authority over Ukrainian lands. Despite the protests of some bad actors today, people have always known that there were real differences between the two. If the early modern rulers of Moscow could not see this, they would never have bothered to go to the Patriarch of Constantinople seeking reassurance regarding the legitimacy of Moscow.

Importantly for later events, the events of 1589 were not the end of Kyiv's supersession by Moscow. In 1686, the Patriarch of Constantinople would issue a *tomos* (or binding synodal decree) granting the Patriarch of Moscow the authority to appoint the Metropolitan of Kyiv, thereby completely ending Kyiv's dependence on Constantinople. It was this decision that the Patriarch of Constantinople would revoke in 2018, setting the course for the events of recent years. But that was all still centuries in the future and in some ways a mere formality. With the displacement of Kyiv as a place of chief ecclesiastical honour in 1589 (and again in 1686), Moscow, for now, had both an emperor and a patriarch – it could thus stake a legitimate claim to be 'the Third Rome', the rightful inheritor of Christian Roman legacy. As such, the Russian state could now style itself as the only remaining defender of the Orthodox faith. This was an idea with consequences that even today are hard to avoid.

Reformation and Enlightenment

The fall of Constantinople and the rise of Moscow exacerbated what had already been a spirit of deep conservatism within the Orthodox world. The sense of a world and a faith that were under ever-present threat, always on the verge of being lost, gave rise to a widely held belief that one must always be distrustful of any change, because any change, no matter how small or seemingly innocuous, could signal the beginning of the end. 'Innovation' quickly became a dirty word in the Christian East. This is one of the reasons that it is a matter of great pride to a certain kind of contemporary Orthodox Christian that 'orthodoxy never experienced the Reformation or the Enlightenment'. This is a declaration made with particular delight, the subtext to which is that, Orthodoxy, free from the modernizing influences of the Reformation and the Enlightenment, has escaped the corrosive effects of modernity itself and that the Orthodox world is one to which modern liberalism remains completely alien. A plausible enough idea, one might think, but in reality one that is clearly and demonstrably untrue.

Orthodox Christian cultures are principally European cultures, even if they remain to some extent on the periphery of Europe. As such, they have not escaped the effects of the great intellectual and social currents of European history, even if their experience has been ever so slightly different. In fact, one might say that it was the arrival of a large number of Orthodox Christians in Western Europe that set in motion the events that gave rise to modernity: to the Renaissance, the Reformation and the Enlightenment. Rather than brave resisters of modernity, it was Orthodox Christians who made modernity possible.

Sophia was not the only Greek refugee who found her way to Western Europe following the fall of Constantinople. Among the ranks of the newly arrived Greek *Romanoi* there were scholars and teachers who carried with them, not only the Greek language, but a deep love and knowledge of the literature and culture of the ancient world. These Byzantine refugees were instrumental in reintroducing all things Greek into Western Europe and, in doing so, added critical fuel to the fires of the Renaissance.

The events of the early modern period highlight the different experiences of history of Eastern and Western Christianity, perhaps beyond even the Crusades. Much of this difference centres around the 'rediscovery' of the ancient, pre-Christian world by Western Europeans, paradoxically with the help of Byzantine scholars. It is one of the great absurdities of history that the fall of Constantinople created the circumstances in which, at the same moment that modern Greek ethnic identity was being forged in the cauldron of Ottoman occupation (an identity that would shape itself primarily around the Orthodox Christian faith and a nostalgia for the lost Christian Empire), in Western Europe the ancient pre-Christian Greeks were becoming a significant cultural icon, the imagined fathers of 'Western Civilization' who embodied all the values and ideals seemingly lost in the newly named 'Dark Ages'. It was at this moment that the entire medieval history of Christendom, so deeply important to the modern people of the Balkans and Eastern Europe (Greek and Russian, Serbian and Romanian), was seemingly erased from the Western mind, creating for those Western people a disconnect between the ideal and the actual with respect to the Christian East – a disconnect that persists to this day.

The early Protestant Reformers were the first to encounter this incongruity. Renaissance humanism, characterized by the study of the Greek language and a desire to rediscover the Scriptures in their original tongue, laid the foundation for the Reformation. Once the Bible was accessible in its original languages, the power of the Roman Church to act as arbiter between the faithful and God was broken. The spirit of inquiry that fuelled the Reformation began and ended in the reformers' rediscovery of Scripture in its original language. As good humanists of the era, they were also very aware of the archetype of 'the Greek': that rational, learned figure who had given birth to all that was good in human society. As good theologians, they had a vague knowledge of 'the Church of the Greeks', an ancient Christian Church, much like that of Rome, that existed outside the authority of the Pope. For many it seemed too good to be true. It is thus an oft-forgotten part of the Reformation that many reformers sought the Orthodox Church, usually the Greeks because of that humanist affinity, not the Russians who were, after all, the only 'free' Orthodox people left in the world.

The most important of these early Reformation–Orthodox dialogues occurred between Lutheran theologians teaching at the University of Tubingen in Germany and Patriarch Jeremias II Tranos of Constantinople between 1575 and 1581 (this is the same patriarch who made Moscow a patriarchal throne). Initiated by the eager Germans, their first move was to translate the Augsburg Confession into Greek and send it to the Patriarch in the Ottoman Empire. Certainly, they concluded, a rational Greek would be in complete agreement with them. They could not have been more wrong. The Patriarch replied by pointing out what he perceived as errors in their theology. Tellingly, the dialogue collapsed primarily around the question of Patristics, and the role that the ancient Fathers of the Church ought to have in the contemporary interpretation of Scripture. Much to the disappointment of the Germans, the Greek Patriarch was not quite willing to abandon the authority of the ancients in the pursuit of his own reasoning.

While Jeremias II was unpersuaded by Protestant arguments, one of his successors was not so resistant. Cyril Lucaris was born in Crete in 1572, while the island was under Venetian control. His studies took him across Europe, including to Wittenberg and Geneva, where he encountered Protestant theologians and came under their influence. There is ample evidence, despite Orthodox protests to the contrary, that he was deeply affected by the Calvinists in Geneva. As Patriarch of Alexandria and later as Patriarch of Constantinople, he sent young Greek men to study at Protestant universities in Switzerland and the northern Low Countries. He corresponded with several key Protestant clerics and theologians, including the Archbishop of Canterbury and, in 1629, he published his theological treatise *Confessio* which, while certainly accommodating Orthodox language and theology, is at its core a Calvinist document. His assassination in 1638, on the order of the Sultan, made him a martyr in the eyes of the Greek Orthodox faithful, who were predisposed to see any enemy of the Sultan as a friend, and he is today venerated as a saint. This makes his problematic theology even more of a problem, although it is a problem frequently brushed over in Eastern Christian circles. However, his life and work make it impossible to deny that Orthodoxy was touched by the Reformation.

Calvinist Patriarchs aside, it is also worth noting that Russia, not bound by the limits of Ottoman Rule, was home not only to Lutherans, Mennonites and others imported from Germany by Catherine the Great, but to many of its own indigenous Protestant-esque movements. From as early as the fourteenth century, Russia witnessed the rise of any number of indigenous dissenting religious communities, such as the Molokan, Dukhoborr and Khlysts, all of whom took up many of the same causes and displayed many of the same characteristics as the Western Protestants. Indeed, one could argue that the fact that a Reformation did not flourish in Russia as it did in the German states was because of political realities, not religious ones. The Protestant Reformation blossomed because competing German princes sought to leverage religion in their battles with each other, repudiating or allying with Rome as served their purposes, and providing safe havens for theologians who ran afoul of the authorities in other domains. For the same reason that the Reformation thrived in the politically fractured German kingdoms and Low Countries, it was quickly stamped out in a unified Spain. As in Spain, in Russia, there was only one tsar and nowhere to flee so long as he remained convinced of the Orthodox faith.

The ideas of the Enlightenment made more headway in Orthodox worlds, however. The Enlightenment, the seventeenth- and eighteenth-century European philosophical and intellectual movement that brought us so many of modernity's most cherished ideals, from constitutional government to scientific rationalism, was not only inspired by the ancient Greeks but also profoundly influenced by contemporary Greeks. Known as the Neo-Hellenic or Modern Greek Enlightenment, the uniquely Orthodox expression of the Enlightenment, which was not confined to Greek speakers but also included Romanians, Serbs, Bulgarians and indeed Russians, has had a major impact on subsequent history, both for Orthodoxy and the world.

The Greek merchant class of the Ottoman Empire accumulated considerable wealth throughout the sixteenth century. By the beginning of the seventeenth century, Ottoman Greeks were using their significant financial resources to send their sons to study in the great capitals of Western Europe, especially Vienna and Paris. Both cities were quickly becoming not only educational and cultural centres, but important sites for the creation and dissemination of the Enlightenment. The young Greek men who arrived in the cities as students were soon exposed to a world filled with ideas about equality, liberty and revolution, ideas revered in ancient Greece, which was seen by many Enlightenment thinkers as an exemplar for modern societies. Their experience as Christian subjects of the Ottoman Empire had furthermore made them deeply aware of the consequences of inequality and injustice in society, and made them particularly open to hearing the Enlightenment's call for equality, tolerance and pluralism.

Many of these students thus began to make their own contributions to Enlightenment discourse. Today, thinkers such as Theophilos Karis, Adamantios Korais and Eugenios Voulgaris remain important figures, not just of modern Greek philosophy but of European philosophy. And the legacy of men such as Rigas Feraios can be seen not just in books and ideas, but in the very existence of the Greek state, because the Greek War of Independence is, in many ways, the greatest child of the Neo-Hellenic Enlightenment. These kinds of revolutionary thought were not safe to have in the Ottoman Empire and it is a very overlooked fact that many of the Orthodox Christian Enlightenment thinkers found their way to Russia and into the courts of Catherine the Great and Peter the Great.

This is not to say that the Enlightenment in the Orthodox context was the same as in the West. This is simply not true. For example, within Orthodox cultures the Enlightenment never took on the strident atheism found in some corners of the radical Enlightenment in the West. In fact, many of the Neo-Hellenic Enlightenment's leading figures were clergy. Their ideas and their engagement with the ideas of others shaped Orthodox theology and, importantly, Orthodox cultures, laying the foundations for the post-Ottoman Orthodox world. To deny that the Enlightenment ever took root within Orthodox minds is to deny a substantial part of both Orthodox and world history, and worse still, it feeds a lie perpetuated by dangerous reactionaries whose chief aim is not to erase eighteenth-century thinkers from the pages of history but to undermine many of the key notions and ideas that grew out of the Enlightenment by painting them as 'having nothing to do with Orthodoxy'.

Nationalism

The existence of nation states among traditionally Orthodox people is the most obvious indicator of the fallacy of the claim that Orthodoxy was unaffected by the Enlightenment and the general political and ideological trends of modernity. Nationalism and the nation state are very much, after all, an outcome of modernity. For most of history, people have lived in large multinational, multi-ethnic empires. Orthodox Christianity was shaped in the context of such an empire. But for the past two centuries, it is not imperialism but nationalism that has been the driving political force in the Orthodox world.

The Greek War of Independence marks an important moment in the history of the Orthodox Christian engagement with the nation state. While it is true that the Western Philhellenes, such as Lord Byron, who came to fight for the Greek cause, were fixed upon the image of ancient Greece being reborn and committed to making Athens the capital of the new Greek nation, the Greek fighters were much more grounded in their Byzantine past and dreamed of fighting on to reclaim Istanbul as a Greek city. The idea of retaking Asia Minor and Constantinople, known as the *Megali Idea* (the Great Idea), persisted well into the twentieth century. (In fact, if you look hard enough you can see pockets of survival even in the twenty-first.)

This zeal to recreate the Byzantine Empire made the Greek Revolution particularly dangerous for the Patriarch of Constantinople. Within a month of the Greeks declaring their independence on 25 March 1821 (the Feast of the Annunciation), on Easter Sunday of that year, the Patriarch of Constantinople, Gregory V, was hanged by the Sultan, accused of supporting the rebellion. His corpse was left to hang for two days. The message was clear and well received by his successor, Jerimias IV, who was quick to condemn the revolutionaries, declaring them not only rebels, but heretics.

Tensions with the Patriarchate persisted, and even intensified, with the establishment of the Greek state. In 1833, the Greek government declared the independence of the Church of Greece from the Ecumenical Patriarchate. This highly irregular and clearly uncanonical act was acknowledged by the Patriarchate in 1850, glad to be rid of his politically problematic Greek brothers. While it was probably not the Patriarch's intention for this singular act to become a precedent, the pattern had been set.

Throughout the nineteenth century, as various nation states emerged in traditionally Orthodox Christian lands, independent ecclesiastical jurisdictions were set up to correspond with the new political borders in line with the Greek model. This became an increasing problem for the Patriarchate of Constantinople, which saw its territory slowly slip away as state after state emerged within the borders of the old empire.

By 1872, the Great Church of Constantinople had had enough. That year the Exarchate of Bulgaria, set up by the Ottomans two years earlier to try to appease nationalist sentiments, unilaterally broke away from Constantinople and declared its independence, a move that happened in parallel with the rise of a nationalist political movement among the Bulgarians. The incumbent Patriarch of Constantinople, Anthimus VI, began to see such nationalist movements as an existential threat to both Christian unity and his own position. In September of 1872, he convened a council at Constantinople for the purpose of condemning what the synod called phyletism:

> We censure, condemn, and declare contrary to the teachings of the Gospel and the sacred canons of the holy Fathers the

> doctrine of phyletism, or the difference of races and national diversity in the bosom of the Church of Christ. (Article I of the Decree of the 1872 Council of Constantinople)

Very seldom has the pronouncement of a synod been so widely misunderstood so quickly. Today, many Orthodox Christians of a more progressive variety point to the Council's declaration as proof that 'racism' is a heresy. It is doubtful, however, that the Ottoman Greek bishops who gathered in 1872 had any concept of race or racism as we understand it today. They were concerned with maintaining the power of the Greek religious authorities in Constantinople, Alexandria and Antioch, and were nervous that the power that they had clung to over centuries of Ottoman rule would be whisked away in a wave of nationalist zeal. The Patriarch's authority was all that was left of the old empire and now nationalism was threatening even that.

Not only was the declaration of the 1872 Council of Constantinople misunderstood, it was also ignored. Within seven years of the Council the creation of an independent Serbian state by the Congress of Berlin led to the founding of the independent Patriarchate of Belgrade.

The problem was even worse in the diaspora. Long lacking any missionary zeal, Orthodox Christianity has largely been found outside of its traditional homeland, where it has travelled in the trunks of immigrants. For these people, as for many other immigrants, the Church was as much a place of ethnic belonging as a religion. At church you could speak your own language, eat your own food, practise your own customs. Moreover, on a purely practical level, no one was really organizing these immigrant churches. The whole thing was an incredibly ad hoc affair, with local communities gathering and writing 'home' for a priest. The priests were, of course, under obedience to their local bishops. Because the period of migration from the

Balkans and Eastern Europe largely coincided with the breakdown of Constantinople's authority, the result was that the newly independent churches, as well the Mother Church, all ended up establishing ethnic outposts around the world.

The result is that, today, in most non-traditionally Orthodox places there are 'overlapping jurisdictions', the very uncanonical state of having bishops who share territory. Of course, being out of step with a medieval organizational chart is not the worst thing that can happen. However, this proliferation of global ethnic churches within the Orthodox world has, particularly of late, had the consequence of creating some very bad marketing for Orthodoxy. In particular, this division along ethnic lines, an accident of nineteenth-century Eastern European politics, has led some contemporary Western racists to find their way into the Orthodox Church. If you were asked to name the top three features that attract members of the Western far right, you would do well to guess homophobia, antisemitism and nationalism. The irony is that at least nationalism has been acknowledged as a destructive force since it first found its way in.

That is not to say that the repudiation of nationalism within the Orthodox context is wholly unproblematic either. Russia's current incursions into its former sphere of influence is theologically and politically aligned with the notion of *Russkiy mir* ("Russian world"). And efforts to repudiate this imperialist agenda are met with charges of phyletism.

For an imperial faith, nationalism was never going to be an easy fit. What could not have been predicted was the extent to which Orthodox people would embrace nationalism with such zeal that, for 200 years and counting, one of the most persistent problems in the Orthodox world would be nationalism and its very troublesome repudiations. Despite all this, nationalism is not the ideology that has had the most destructive consequences for Orthodoxy. That ideology really did come from the West.

Communism

If it comes as a surprise to some in the West that Russia is a country with a long and complex Christian history, this is no doubt because, for the bulk of the twentieth century, 'Holy Russia' lay confined within the officially atheist USSR and 'Godless Russia' was made the stuff of schoolchildren's nuclear nightmares. A great deal of ink has been spilled in the quest to discover why traditionally Orthodox countries were more susceptible to Communist revolution and why they have been so much slower than their traditionally Catholic counterparts to recover from the ill effects of the Communist era. It seems unlikely that one clear and definitive answer to either question will ever be found. What is clear is that the great modern trauma of Orthodox Christianity is the Communist era, which inflicted in 70 years nearly as much psychological damage as the Ottomans managed in 500. This is no doubt because, unlike the Ottoman occupation which came from outside, the horrors of the Communist era emerged from within.

This is not to say that there has not been a long-standing attempt to lay blame at someone, anyone else's feet, feeding on the Orthodox world's pervasive xenophobia. And it is not uncommon to this day to hear the Bolshevik Revolution blamed on Jewish people, the Freemasons, the British and just about anyone else other than the pious, suffering faithful of an Orthodox nation.

As part of the impulse to cast the Communist era as an external threat as opposed to an internal malfunction, much of the Orthodox narrative of the Communist era today focuses on the martyrs produced and the persecution endured at the hands of 'the Communists'. The fact that there was indeed genuine persecution of Christians and also of the institutional Church is, in some times and in some places, used as a shield by Church officials and apologists to set the institutional Church apart from other societal institutions, the vast majority of which have been tainted by the Communist period. And to be clear, Christians, like all religious people, did face serious repression and punishment under Communism, and many faithful people, including the clergy, found themselves imprisoned or executed. Church property was seized, parishes closed and ancient basilicas and monasteries were destroyed; however, the attitude of Communist officials towards the Church, and more importantly the involvement of Church officials with Communist governments, varied across time and place. And there were times when, calling on Orthodoxy's long history of co-operation with the Russian Empire, Orthodox clerics found themselves acting in harmony with the atheist state. While acknowledging that each history is unique, the Russian experience demonstrates in stark terms the complexity of Church resistance and co-operation with a Communist regime, a pattern that was repeated across the Orthodox world in the twentieth century.

Before the Russian Revolution, the Russian Orthodox Church enjoyed a uniquely privileged position in Russian life, a position it had gained through the tsars' attempts to recreate the Roman Empire along the banks of the Volga. In the instant of revolution, the Church saw all of that power slip away. And when the Bolsheviks declared a separation of Church and state, the Russian Orthodox Church became the first Orthodox Church ever to exist without any state support. It was by no means the worst thing that would happen to the Church under the Bolsheviks, but it was a psychological trauma that would foreshadow things to come and inform the actions of clerical officials in the coming years and decades. In the past there had been times when the Patriarch and the Emperor would squabble and even get to the point of all-out war with each other. But the notion that the Church and her clerics would simply exist outside of, and even in direct opposition to, the state was simply unthinkable in an Orthodox context.

The defeat of the White Army in the Russian Civil War of 1917–1922 eliminated the Church's last hope of returning to its former position of prominence. Lenin, for his part, loathed religion and believed that the only correct way to deal with the Church was to mercilessly suppress it. The first years of Communist rule brought about the worst period of persecution that the Church would endure. Within the first five years of the Bolshevik government, 28 bishops and 1,200 priests were executed. In 1921, the tenth Congress of the Communist Party of the Soviet Union convened. Chief among the congress's aims was stamping out religion, and Orthodoxy in particular, once and for all. When Patriarch Tikhon died in 1925, the Soviet officials forbade the election of a new patriarch. Following his death, a metropolitan bishop, Peter (Polyansky) of Krutitsy, was selected to serve as *patriarchal locum tenens*, but he was arrested just eight months later. He had, like Patriarch Tikhon, left a list of three possible successors. At the time of his arrest, the only name on the list that belonged to a person not in prison was Sergius of Nizhny Novgorod. Sergius, who had been imprisoned himself between 30 November 1926 and 27 March 1927, began to search for a way to make the active persecution end.

On 29 July 1927, Sergius, now acting *patriarchal locum tenens,* issued the now infamous encyclical *Epistle to the Pastors and their Flocks,* in which he called on the Orthodox faithful to demonstrate uncompromising loyalty to and co-operation with the Soviet regime. This was the beginning of what has been derisively termed 'Sergeism', a policy of co-operation with the Soviet government that did not pay off until the Second World War. Then, as German tanks rolled toward Russia, the Soviet authorities began their rapprochement with the Orthodox Church. In need of the Church's support, Stalin scaled back his persecution, finally accepting the olive branch offered by Serigus over a decade before. Imprisoned clergy were released, church property was returned and the Moscow Theological Seminary and Academy was allowed to reopen. From this point forward, the Russian Orthodox Church would be allowed to operate within the Soviet state, if not free, then as least not as the victim of open persecution.

The taste of being back in the state's good grace was too much to resist. The post-war Russian Orthodox Church went all in on its strategy of appeasement and co-operation. It largely abandoned a traditionalist orientation, praising the reforms of the Soviet government to social and cultural life. Frequently, Church officials were in open collusion with the Soviet state. This open complicity only grew worse when a period of revived persecution under Nikita Khrushchev resulted in large numbers of Russian clergy being replaced by KGB operatives. By the late 1960s and early 1970s the Patriarch of Moscow was winning Soviet medals for his contributions to international peace.

It is worth noting that much of the current leadership of the Russian Orthodox Church came of age during this period of co-operation with the Soviet state, and it is difficult to disentangle all the ways that this experience inevitably shaped them as clergy and as men. For example, an investigation by two Swiss newspapers, *Le Matin Dimanche* and *Sonntagzeitung*, has recently unveiled that, according to documents in the Swiss Federal Archive, Patriarch Kirill, the current head of the Russian Church, was working for the KGB when he lived in Geneva in the early 1970s, where he had officially be sent to serve as a representative of the Russian Orthodox Church on the World Council of Churches.

In the Russian Orthodox diaspora, beyond the Iron Curtain, the Russian Church's capitulation to the Soviet regime was unthinkable. Cut off from Moscow, diaspora Russian churches sought to find a way to understand themselves in this new era. While many were either co-operative or passive in their resistance, some of the faithful abroad entered into open rebellion against the Soviet state and their lackey clerics. The most prominent example of this more aggressive stance is that of the Russian Orthodox Church Outside of Russia (ROCOR).

Established in the early 1920s by Russians in exile after the Revolution, the ROCOR was defined by its clergy's decision to refuse to co-operate when Sergius sent word from Moscow that they were to be obedient to him and, by extension, the Soviet state. This is not to say that the ROCOR bishops and priests had suddenly become Anabaptists. The ROCOR faithful hated the Soviet government for its atheism and attacks on the Church and traditional Russian culture. They did not, however, hate state power, as evidenced by the arguably close and now deeply embarrassing relationship that the ROCOR maintained with Adolf Hitler and his Nazi regime. For example, in 1938, Metropolitan Anastassy, the highest-ranking cleric in the ROCOR, sent a letter to the Fuhrer thanking him for his support and for allowing a Russian parish to be opened in Berlin. While there have been, even as late as 2002, attempts by the ROCOR to excuse Anastassy's response to Hitler, claiming that he could have had no real knowledge of the Nazi Party's inner workings or objectives, it is worth noting that 1938 was the very year in which Nazi policy towards Jewish people became openly radicalized. It was the year of Kristallnacht. The suggestion that the Metropolitan was unaware of Nazi objectives in 1938 reads more like an insult to his intelligence than a defence of his virtue.

As the Cold War chilled and the Russian Orthodox Church's relationship with the Soviets warmed, the ROCOR became more defiant in its opposition. Embracing a social and liturgical conservatism with an intensity not previously seen in the diaspora, ROCOR set about preserving what had been destroyed in their homeland. The ROCOR was a Church and a community defined by its stubborn refusal to co-operate with the Soviet state or with their brothers who would choose such accommodation. Drawing on Orthodoxy's old sense of siege, the ROCOR hunkered down for the duration. In his will, Metropolitan Anastassy wrote as close to a mission statement as the ROCOR would ever have:

> As regards the Moscow Patriarchate and its hierarchs, then, so long as they continue in close, active and benevolent cooperation with the Soviet Government, which openly professes its complete godlessness and strives to implant atheism in the entire Russian nation, then the Church Abroad, maintaining Her purity, must not have any canonical, liturgical or even simply external communion with them whatsoever, leaving each one of them at the same time to the final judgment of the Council (Sobor) of the future free Russian Church.
> *The Last Will and Testament of Metropolitan Anastassy* (1957)

'Maintaining Her purity' – that was the goal of the ROCOR, a goal one might argue it has shared with the conservative forces within Orthodoxy for a millennium. The fear of contamination from outside sources – the Christian West, liberalism, Communism – looms large in the Orthodox mind and has done for centuries, from the time that conflict with the Latin Church sent the East into a hyperfocus on 'maintaining the Tradition' (or perhaps the purity of that tradition – or both). Communism and the experience of Communism only exacerbated these tendencies, demonstrating what had been long feared: it really could all be washed away in a single moment.

Which brings us to today

The collapse of Communism in the early 1990s marked a moment of both opportunity and tension in the Orthodox world. It is important to consider that, after seven decades of official atheism, it was not self-evident that the Church would enjoy any of the power or influence it had exerted before the upheavals of the twentieth century. Moreover, if there was going to be a place for religion in the new East Europe, Orthodoxy was going to have to compete with other traditions.

In the immediate aftermath of the end of Communism, American missionaries streamed into Russia and the former Eastern Bloc. It is unclear whether these missionaries knew that, prior to the Revolution, Russia had been a deeply and overwhelmingly Christian nation for centuries or whether they simply did not consider Orthodox Christians, with their gold-clad bishops, ubiquitous icons and chanted liturgies, to be sufficiently Christian. In fairness, and if other Western engagements with Orthodoxy are taken into account, then it was probably a combination of both.

The missionaries arrived with plenty of US dollars in their pockets, financial support that the Orthodox churches of the region desperately needed. The Patriarch of Moscow, Alexius II, saw the opportunities these missionaries presented and began to forge a friendship. It was a fateful decision. Throughout the 1990s and early 2000s, American missionaries were largely responsible for providing Bibles and catechism materials to the Russian Orthodox Church; a rather shocking reality for a faith tradition so long suspicious of outside, and particularly Western influence. For their part, the American Evangelicals in

Moscow were doubtless beginning to understand that they had found an ally and perhaps a kindred spirit.

They were not the first conservative American Protestants to notice this. Beginning in the late 1970s, a not insignificant number of highly conservative American Protestants, both Evangelical and mainline, had found their way into the Orthodox Church in America. Largely converting to the Arab-tradition Antiochian Orthodox Christian Archdioceses (ACOCA) of America and the Russian-tradition Orthodox Church in America (OCA), these converts were attracted to these parishes largely because, unlike the churches of the Greek and Serbian diaspora, the liturgy was celebrated in English. These new Orthodox believers were largely, although not exclusively, fleeing the progressive reforms of their own former traditions (in the case of the mainline Protestants) or looking for a faith tradition that mirrored their increasingly more reactionary politics (in the case of Evangelicals). By the early 2000s, American converts made up 70 per cent of the ACOCA and 50 per cent of the OCA, transforming these jurisdictions from the immigrant communities that had defined the Orthodox diaspora to what one can only see as ideologically driven religious outposts in which (more in keeping with the currents of American history than Orthodox tradition) people gathered to worship based on shared political ideology rather than on a common ethnic or spiritual heritage. Contact with the American Religious Right, both at home and abroad, has transformed the Orthodox Church, drawing Global Orthodoxy increasingly into contemporary Culture Wars.

In 2009, Patriarch Kirill of Moscow and All Rus came to the apostolic throne of Moscow. This was a fortuitous choice for Putin. In 1993, Patriarch Kirill had founded the World Russian People's Council, an international policy forum, which has become one of the chief platforms for promoting the concept of *Russkiy mir* and other policy objectives of the reactionary elements within the Russian church and state, both at home and abroad. Nine years into the Putin era, that these two ambitious men would occupy their posts at the same moment marked a turning point. Patriarch Kirill and Vladimir Putin have worked in tandem, like the emperors and patriarchs of old, to promote their shared ambitions. In doing so, they have pursued a policy that has sought to position Russia as a revived world power in terms of both military aggression (as in Ukraine and Georgia) and through the exercise of soft power as a global moral leader (as in the case of the Russian Orthodox Church's participation in the World Congress of Families).

It is a policy that has brought Russia into conflict with the world. It also a policy that has brought the Russian Orthodox Church into conflict with parts of the wider Orthodox world. The Putin–Kirill Pact will only be successful if the Russian Orthodox Church, headed by Patriarch Kirill, can position themselves as the undisputed leaders of Orthodoxy. In this quest, Patriarch Kirill's chief rival is Bartholomew I, Patriarch of Constantinople. Born on the island of Imbros (Turkish: Gökçeada), Patriarch Bartholomew has followed in the footsteps of his predecessors over the past 100 years by seeking to establish the Patriarchate of Constantinople as the global head of Orthodoxy in the Church, thus securing his position within the Turkish state. While Patriarch Kirill has pursued his goals by aligning himself with the most reactionary forces in the world today, Patriarch Bartholomew has, some might say, chosen to pursue what is, for an Orthodox cleric, a notably progressive agenda. He has made environmental protection a major plank of his episcopacy and has advocated for pluralism and religious tolerance, positions that are no doubt partly born from his precarious position within Turkey.

Since 2018, when Patriarch Bartholomew, at the behest of the post-Maidan Ukrainian government, established the Orthodox Church of Ukraine, the two patriarchs have been acting in open hostility toward each other, and, following their lead, the various factions of the already fractured Orthodox world have lined up on their respective sides. This conflict has only been intensified by the war in Ukraine and many are now worried that it will develop into a definitive and enduring schism between Moscow and Constantinople (and their respective spheres of influence).

What follows here is a record of this period in Orthodox history, a moment of existential crisis for the Orthodox Church. For Orthodoxy, the past is not just a prologue, it is the opening sentence of every chapter, the theme on every page. Whatever happens next, it will inevitably happen in the shadow of a long and haunting history.

Part 2

WHO IS PATRIARCH KIRILL AND WHY IS HE DANGEROUS?

August 29, 2018

Introducing Putin's greatest admirer

It sounds like something from the days of the tsars: at the height of Stalin's terror, a humble priest serving in Leningrad's Transfiguration Cathedral, baptized an infant in secret. Many such secret baptisms occurred throughout the Soviet period, but this one would turn out to be historic. The priest was Father Michael Gundyayev, whose son would become Patriarch Kirill of Moscow, the leader of the Russian Orthodox Church. The baby was Vladimir Putin.

This strange story was first told as part of the Russian state TV documentary *Patriarch* and, while technically possible, seems an unlikely coincidence. The factual nature of the story is not entirely relevant, however, because it points to a greater truth: that the Russian Church and the Russian state have resumed their marriage.

In the era of Putin, the Russian Orthodox Church has resumed much of its former imperial role as a servant of the state. And in a time of renewed Russian confidence and aggression abroad, the Russian Orthodox Church has become an important instrument of state power. This is a development with dangerous implications, not only for the global Orthodox Church, but for human rights and political freedom around the world.

Patriarch Kirill has described the Putin era as a 'miracle from God', and offered his powerful opposition to the pro-democracy protests in Moscow in 2012. He has frequently supported government policy in sermons and on state-run television, positioning Russia in the role of spiritual defender in response to Western objections to Russian human rights policy: 'We have been through an epoch of atheism, and we know what it is to live without God. We want to shout to the whole world, "Stop"!' His 2011 book, *Freedom and Responsibility*, posits a contemporary political landscape in which two antagonistic world-views – one liberal, secular and humanistic, the other religious and traditional – are engaged in an existential battle.

The idea of a mortal battle against the forces of secularism has found ready ears among some of the most reactionary corners of the West. The popularity of Orthodoxy among white nationalists in the USA, for example, has significant overtones of pro-Russian – and perhaps more importantly, pro-Kirill – sentiment.

But one does not even need to look as far as self-proclaimed white nationalists to see the influence of Patriarch Kirill and the Russian Orthodox Church. In addition to its popularity among many mainstream American Evangelicals, the Russian Church has been an important pillar of Steve Bannon's coalition of Christian traditionalists. These budding alliances, with access to the highest levels of American government and power, are why the hacking revelations are concerning.

There can be little doubt that the Russian Church is now (once again) an active and potentially aggressive arm of the Russian state. The Russian state will act to protect its interests and the Church will act in the interests of the state. In fact, as can be seen in Ukraine, these interests are often deeply intertwined.

This, in itself, would not be a problem, or of any particular interest for those outside the Orthodox Church, if not for the global non-Orthodox alliances into which the Russian patriarch has led his Church. These alliances, combined with acts of Russian state aggression, can only be seen as concrete efforts to undermine liberal democracy around the world. And that should be of concern to everyone.

March 6, 2020

What's so scary about the inclusion of 'God' in the Russian constitution?

Last Friday, The US House of Representatives' Tom Lantos Commission on Human Rights heard testimony that Russia's human rights record, including its record on religious freedom, is worsening. There were few surprises in Elizabeth Cassidy's testimony – particularly for those who have been paying even the most passing attention to the Putin regime's power grab both at home and abroad. Cassidy, the director of research and policy at the U.S. Commission on International Religious Freedom (USCIRF), told the Congressional commission: 'The Russian government maintains, frequently updates and enforces an array of laws that restrict religious freedom . . . These violations are escalating, spreading through the country and even across its borders.'

Indeed, USCIRF has 'been calling for the designation of Russia as a [Country of Particular Concern] since 2017 . . . given the Russian government's repressive activities both in Russia and abroad', reads an USCIRF statement from December. President Trump's State Department has thus far refused to do so, and the reality is that the worst might be yet to come.

Earlier this year, Russian President Vladimir Putin announced that he would seek major changes to the Russian Constitution. Most of the media coverage rightly focused on what such reforms would mean for Putin's future at the country's helm (there is little doubt that the primary motivation for these reforms was to allow Putin to remain in power beyond the 2022 expiration of his presidential term). However, the opening of Russia's first democratic constitution to significant structural overhaul poses other dangers as well. There have been more than 300 proposed changes to the constitution, many of which have serious implications for human rights and religious freedom in the country.

In his 2 February column for the Russian-language service of the German newspaper Deutsche Welle, Patriarch Kirill of Moscow, the head of the Russian Orthodox Church, and a man considered by most to be an ally of Putin, called for 'God' to be mentioned in the new preamble. On the surface, this is not a particularly alarming request. While Ukraine is, to date, alone among post-Soviet states in including a reference to God in its constitution, many more liberal states do so, including Germany, Canada, Ireland, Sweden and Switzerland. In these instances, the constitutional reference to God is frequently a nod to a country's shared religious heritage and does little to undermine the principles of secularism and pluralism upon which modern liberal democracy is built. Arguably, such references in fact enforce these values, by offering the seal of divine imprimatur to the legal foundations of the nation. In the case of Russia, however, this is a suggestion that takes on a much more sinister tone.

The Russian Orthodox Church has, to say the least, a bad track record on issues of political liberty and civil rights. Patriarch Kirill himself rather infamously declared in 2016 that 'some human rights are heresy'. The Russian Orthodox Church, including close deputies of the Patriarch, were intimately involved in the 2017 law that decriminalized domestic violence in Russia, as well as the 2013 'gay propaganda' law that has been a major force for the state persecution of LGBTQ people in Russia. Furthermore, Patriarch Kirill and the Russian Orthodox Church he leads have worked hard to develop close alliances with illiberal forces around the world, including Franklin Graham, Steve Bannon and the World Congress of Families.

In fact, it would not be going too far to say that the arch-conservative positions of Kirill's Russian Orthodox Church operate as an instrument of Russian soft power, drafting reactionary forces around the world onto the Russian side. It is, for instance, difficult not to see the Patriarch's ongoing ecclesiastical conflict with the Greek Orthodox Patriarch of Constantinople, focused on hotspots such as Ukraine and Western Europe, through the lens of Russia's increasingly aggressive foreign policy and its desire not only to cause chaos in Western democracies, but to undermine the fundamental trust in liberalism and pluralism that underlies their success.

It is in this light that the seemingly innocuous request of a bishop that 'God' be included in the preamble of his nation's constitution takes on a significantly more sinister tone. And it should, for any honest observer, raise serious concerns about the failure of liberalism to have taken root in post-Soviet Russia and the country's ever deeper slide into totalitarianism.

Moreover, given Russia's aggressive foreign posture, one that is not just military or political but also distinctly cultural, those invested in the larger project of global democracy should also be worried. One of the cornerstones of contemporary Russian foreign policy is to undermine the faith of those living in liberal, pluralist societies in the effectiveness, stability and frankly goodness of their values and institutions. This is an objective that has been all too appealing to the Russian Orthodox Church, and particularly its current leader. If Russia ceases to be simply an authoritarian state and becomes increasingly theocratic in its authoritarianism, there could be greater trouble ahead for us all.

Russia has never been a country synonymous with liberty. Authoritarianism is as native to her as her birch forests. But there is evidence that things are getting worse, and that the Russian Orthodox Church is renewing its ancient role as the handmaiden of Russian state power. And that is something that should concern anyone worried about the future of liberalism, particularly in places where it has historically been much more successful than Russia.

February 21, 2022

Make no mistake, if there's a war between Russia and Ukraine, it will be a religious war

Putin has now ordered Russian troops into Donetsk and Luhansk. The first major conflict between two Orthodox Christian nations since the War of the Stray Dog in 1925 has just begun. That conflict (the resolution of which was, incidentally, perhaps the only significant accomplishment of the League of Nations) was clearly and plainly a territorial dispute. On its surface, so is the current conflict in Ukraine. But appearances can be deceptive. Make no mistake about it, if there is a war between Russia and Ukraine, it will be a religious war. The sooner those in the West recognize this reality and catch up on the details the better.

There is a very recent precedent for this. In the early part of this century, in the aftermath of 9/11, the rise of Islamic fundamentalism was – to be clear, quite justifiably – given a significant amount of attention. At the same time, many rushed to assure the world that those young men who flew planes into buildings and stoned unveiled women in the street did not represent 'the real Islam'.

Far fewer made the much more accurate observation that both Osama bin Laden and Abdolkarim Soroush represent real and legitimate positions within Islam, because traditions are complicated and people with vastly differing world-views can, with credibility, lay claim to the same historical community. If you need further proof of this, remember that both Greg Locke (who believes witches have infiltrated his church) and Leshia Evans (who peacefully stared down police at a protest of the killings of Alton Sterling and Philando Castile) are both devout Christians.

This reality sometimes leads to conflict, particularly in historical epochs characterized by significant change and instability. Western Christianity saw its tensions boil over during the Protestant Reformation and the subsequent Counter-Reformation, which not only resulted in permanent fissures within Western Christendom, but the Thirty Years' War, which killed between 25 and 40 per cent of the entire German population.

These conflicts also provided much of the ideological impetus for modern European colonialism, as a depleted Catholic Church went out in search of new converts (as did the Spanish Conquistadors) and self-assured Calvinists (as did the Pilgrims of Plymouth) went looking for land on which to build their new Jerusalem, as a result of which many non-Western Europeans suffered and died.

Similarly, the tensions that motivated the terrorists in New York, Paris and London, were largely internal to Islam, festering trouble as to how Muslims ought to respond to Western modernity, after centuries outside, and frequently in opposition to its powerful allure. As the uprisings of the Arab Spring suggested, the conflicts of the early twenty-first century were not a 'clash of civilizations', but a clash within a civilization, the crescendo of a 40-year conflict.

This same drama is being played out within Orthodox Christianity at this very moment. Just like Muslims, Orthodox Christians have spent the better part of the modern age in an uncomfortable dance with the West. Throughout this time, Orthodox Christians have disagreed about what their relationship should be with the liberal, secular, rationalist world. And this conflict has come to a head, breaking along old ethnic and national lines that have so long defined identity in the Orthodox world.

February 25, 2022

No, Patriarch Kirill is not calling for peace. In fact, he's Putin's accomplice

Patriarch Kirill of Moscow and All Rus is not calling for peace in Ukraine, and the fact that some in the Western media seem to think he has done so is evidence of how much the West has to learn about Orthodox Christianity, Church–state relations in Russia and Kirill himself.

The first time the leader of the Russian Orthodox Church spoke after Russian troops entered Ukraine (but before fighting had officially begun) was during the commemoration for Defender of the Fatherland Day (known, before 1993, as Red Army Day) when Kirill offered a long, nationalist sermon in which he described the 'sacred border of Russia' and called our era a 'time of peace' – which seems quite inexplicable considering events at the time.

At the exact moment Putin announced the 'special military operation' in (i.e. invasion of) Ukraine, Kirill issued a toothless statement that not only failed to plainly call for the end of violence, but actually restated the historical justification for the invasion that had been offered by Vladimir Putin earlier in the week. This should not be too surprising as it is the same version of history Kirill has used before to argue against the independence of the Ukrainian Orthodox Church and in favour of keeping Ukrainian Orthodox Christians under the yoke of Moscow.

Kirill's tepid remarks also stand in contrast to the words of other Orthodox hierarchs. The Ecumenical Patriarch Bartholomew of Constantinople, for example, called the invasion an unprovoked attack and a violation of human rights. Patriarch Daniel of Romania called the violence 'a war launched by Russia against a sovereign and independent state'. Even Metropolitan Onufry, the head of the Ukrainian Orthodox Church that is still tied to the Moscow Patriarchate – literally, Kirill's Man in Kyiv – compared the Russian invasion to Cain killing his brother Abel and addressed Putin directly.

This difference has not gone unnoticed by those in Russia and Ukraine and throughout the Eastern Christian world. In the words of Sergei Chapnin, editor-in-chief of *The Gifts*, writing at *Public Orthodoxy*:

> Today it is abundantly clear: Patriarch Kirill is not ready to defend his flock—neither the people of Ukraine nor the people of Russia—against Putin's aggressive regime. Human suffering is not one of his priorities.

Every year, Orthodox Christians around the world observe Forgiveness Sunday, the final day before Lent. On this day, the liturgical practice remembers the expulsion of Adam and Eve from Eden and calls on individual believers to repent of their sins against others. The period of repentance and fasting ahead would be the ideal occasion for Patriarch Kirill to exercise the authority of Orthodox hierarchs to concretely condemn and punish the aggressors in this situation. He could, in effect, issue his own religious sanctions, cutting Putin, his government, military leaders and even ordinary soldiers off from the Eucharist.

But he will not do that. Because Patriarch Kirill is an accomplice to Vladimir Putin and has made the Russian Orthodox Church (once again) an agent of state power. The fact that some in the West are not able to plainly see this is to their detriment, because it blinds them from seeing how power is operating in Russia and beyond. It is nice to think that the head of the Russian Orthodox Church is calling for peace, but he is in fact doing nothing beyond the bare minimum and his complicity is encouraging the aggressors in this catastrophe.

I was raised an Orthodox Christian in the West. As a product of the Orthodox diaspora, I am intimately aware of the misunderstandings and misperceptions on both sides. As is nearly always the case, the ignorance is much greater on the Western side – the dominant power always feels that it needs less information about others. But the invasion of Ukraine and the unbridled aggression of a decidedly Orthodox Russia has made this ignorance no longer acceptable. Patriarch Kirill is not calling for peace. That, at least, can no longer be missed.

February 28, 2022

What are the 'evil forces' ranged against Russia and the Russian Church?

If it were not already blatantly obvious that Patriarch Kirill of Moscow is not 'calling for peace', he is now describing Russia's opponents – in its unprovoked, illegal invasion of the Ukraine – as 'evil forces', telling the faithful:

> God forbid that the current political situation in brotherly Ukraine should be aimed at ensuring that the evil forces that have always fought against the unity of Russia and the Russian Church prevail.

While it seems obvious to many that the 'evil forces' to whom the head of the Russian Orthodox Church is referring must be clearly and exclusively the West – or perhaps modernity writ large – a quick survey of Russian history suggests that the 'evil forces' to which Kirill is referring are principally none other than the Jewish people, a strange assertion indeed about a war that is ostensibly about 'de-Nazifying' a country.

Vladimir Putin and Patriarch Kirill share a vision of history in which Ukraine does not exist as a distinct nation or an independent state. To their way of thinking, the tenth-century conversion of the Kyivan Rus forever unites Russians and Ukrainians as a single people, rightly ruled (since the sixteenth century apparently) from Moscow. It is a vision that Kirill stresses in the very sentence in which he invokes 'evil forces': 'brotherly Ukraine' is followed by 'the unity of Russia'.

The idea that Jews are working to undermine Christian unity, or rather unity between Christian people, has a long history, particularly in Orthodoxy and especially in Russia. Centuries of attempts to eradicate or assimilate the Jewish population of the Russian Empire were grounded in the idea that Jewish people not only threatened national homogeneity by their mere existence, but were also actively working to undermine unity since, the thinking went, a truly successful Christian empire would jeopardize Jewish control of the world.

While Patriarch Kirill talks about 'evil forces' undermining Russia's brotherly unity with Ukraine, a Jewish Ukrainian president just happens to lead the resistance to the Russian invasion. Putin knows exactly what he is doing: he is recalling ancient prejudice. He is stirring up the anxiety of conspiracy theorists with theories much older than QAnon.

To be clear, Patriarch Kirill has no great love for liberal democracy or secular pluralism – this is, after all, a man who argued that the concept of human rights is a heresy. But neither does he hold a world-view in which a Christian civilization – a brotherly unity – merely collapses on its own. In his mind, there is always a source of that collapse, and he comes from a cultural tradition in which Jewish people have long been accused of being that source. Now, his country is fighting with a Jewish leader for territory Kirill believes politically and spiritually should rightfully be united with Russia. Clearly, he believes he knows who the problem is. He knows the 'evil forces' at work.

The biggest mistake that those in the West could make about the current conflict is to believe that this conflict can be seen through contemporary Western eyes alone. The Orthodox world has a distinct history and therefore distinct motifs and archetypes that it recalls. This is one such instance. So, again, no, Patriarch Kirill is not calling for peace. In fact, he is activating old antisemitic hatreds that could make the conflict a whole lot worse.

March 7, 2022

Now Kirill blames the war on Western Gay Pride parades

Today is Clean Monday, the first day of the Orthodox Christian Lent. Yesterday was Forgiveness Sunday, a day traditionally dedicated to reflecting upon one's own sins and preparing for and anticipating the long period of fasting and repentance encouraged by the Church for centuries. The homilies preached on Forgiveness Sunday have a long and important history within Orthodox Christianity, and many stand as turning points in the history of Orthodox nations and peoples. To wit, it was on Forgiveness Sunday 1861 that Metropolitan Philaret of Moscow (now canonized) announced that the brutal, centuries-long practice of serfdom had been abolished.

So one can be forgiven for having some expectations of Patriarch Kirill, the current leader of the Russian Orthodox Church – even though he has proven a disappointment since Russia began its war of aggression in Ukraine, in which people who are (by his own assertion) all members of his flock have killed one another and threatened some of Orthodox Christianity's most sacred sites.

Instead, Patriarch Kirill took the occasion of Forgiveness Sunday 2022 to launch a bizarre rant, at the iconic Cathedral of Christ the Saviour in Moscow, asserting that the fighting in Ukraine was a result of the rejection of 'fundamental values' by those who 'claim world power'. These nefarious powers, the Patriarch went on to explain, 'demand that you hold gay pride parades as a test of loyalty'. Countries that fail to take this Rainbow Oath are apparently denied access to Visa, Mastercard and Netflix.

The war in Ukraine, according to the spiritual leader of the Russian Orthodox Church, is one of 'metaphysical significance'. It is a battle between good and evil in which Russia is the last powerful guardian of the good, seeking to maintain God's Holy Laws while the decadent rest are just trying to hold a gay pride parade in Kyiv.

While Patriarch Kirill's sermon was shocking, it wasn't surprising to anyone familiar with the Russian Orthodox Church. This sermon is the natural outcome of rhetoric coming out of the Patriarchate of Moscow, not only over the past decade, but over the past five centuries as well. In recent times, Patriarch Kirill and Vladimir Putin have worked diligently to position the Russian Orthodox Church, and by extension Russia, as leader of the Global Christian Right. And thanks partly to American evangelicals, anti-LGBTQ rhetoric is a hallmark of this worldwide ideological movement. Certainly, anti-LGBTQ laws in Russia and the horrific persecution of gay men in Chechnya (a Russian client state), to which Putin and Kirill turned a blind eye, prove this is, horrifyingly, more than rhetoric. But Kirill's remarks go beyond a decade of horrific anti-LGBTQ repression and the Russian–American Evangelical Lovefest.

For centuries, arguably since the Crusaders' Sack of Constantinople, Orthodox Christianity has shaped its self-conception around the image of the Suffering Servant. Orthodox Christians and Orthodox Christian nations, this logic goes, are the last bastion of true Christianity and pious Christian life. As such, they are bound to suffer at the hands of those who have abandoned the True Faith and who have, like the Prodigal Son in Christ's parable, sought debauched living in 'foreign lands'.

It was from this myth that so much of Orthodox Christian hostility to Western modernity was born. And it is this story that animates the reactionary faction within Orthodoxy's current intra-religious conflict, a faction for which Patriarch Kirill undoubtedly serves as leader.

What is incredibly important to remember is that, in this paradigm, Russia is not the enemy of the West; Moscow is the Third Rome. Vladimir Putin as neo-quasi-emperor is the rightful inheritor of the Roman Empire and of Christendom. In many ways, Patriarch Kirill is not saying that Russia must fight and destroy the West, he is arguing that Russia is the rightful leader of the West.

This is a world-view that obviously can seem shocking to those in Western Europe and North America who have been taught a very different version of history, one that sees the centre of Western power and culture moving from Rome to Madrid to Paris to London to Washington. It is, however, a view of history not shared by everyone. As we painfully found out in the early part of this century, different civilizations have different narratives of the past. Failure to understand the Islamic view of history was a grave fault of the Western powers. Today, the same could be said of the Orthodox view of history. For example, if you have never heard of the Crusaders' Sack of Constantinople in 1204 mentioned above, now is the time to learn.

Yesterday, Patriarch Kirill was talking to the home crowd, both in Russia and beyond. And while it was truly bizarre to blame the Russian invasion of Ukraine on gay pride parades (no amount of expertise or familiarity will make it less so), it does make sense given the history of the Russian Orthodox Church. It is time we all learn more about that history.

April 4, 2022

The Russian Patriarch just gave his most dangerous speech yet – and almost no one in the West has noticed

There is little doubt that Russian Orthodox Patriarch Kirill's Forgiveness Sunday Sermon last month received more attention than any Orthodox cleric's sermon has received in the Western media in a long time. Beyond its frightening absurdity, it is likely this attention is due, in no small part, to its use of culture war rhetoric with which Western audiences are so familiar and about which they are so passionate.

Therefore, it is not necessarily surprising that yesterday's sermon, delivered in the imposing and threatening Cathedral of the Armed Forces, is receiving less attention, although this sermon was arguably far more dangerous and might provide critical insight into what will come next for Russia, Ukraine and the rest of us.

The Fourth Sunday in Lent is dedicated to the commemoration of St John Climacus (also known as St John of the Ladder) in the Eastern Christian tradition. Little is known about this early Desert Father, except that he is the author of one of Christianity's most important ascetical texts, *The Ladder of Divine Ascent*. Divided into thirty parts, the treatise is meant to be a guidebook to a Christian life, with topics ranging from lying to the remembrance of death.

Patriarch Kirill ostensibly took St John of the Ladder and his famed text as the basis for his sermon. And if we're being frank, the first half of the sermon was a fairly benign, if not predictable, standard sermon from a Christian minister. Kirill even reminded his audience: 'The greatest and holiest feeling God has given to man is the feeling of love.' A sentiment that, tragically, sounds hollow coming from a warmongering patriarch.

However, about halfway through, the sermon took a turn for the shocking and dangerous. This occurred at about the point that he acknowledged where he stood: in a cathedral built not so much for the glory of God as for the glory of Russian military might. Here, the Patriarch said he had come to address the leaders of their Russian forces, and through them, their troops. He reminded the assembled congregation of Vladimir Putin's favourite propaganda point in this war: that Russia was fighting fascism in Ukraine just as it had in the Second World War. Then, the Patriarch, whose office was just a few centuries ago (a blink of the eye in the memory of the Christian East) located not in Moscow, but Kyiv, offered up a version of history that simply erases Ukraine from the map. Kirill blames 'various forces' (i.e. outsiders, including – one would imagine – the West) that emerged in the Middle Ages for what he regards as a false division between Russia and Ukraine. In fact, he does not even acknowledge there are such people as Ukrainians, referring to all involved parties (including, perhaps, one could speculate, Belarusians) as 'Holy Russians'.

Disregarding for a moment how simply, factually, wrong Patriarch Kirill's version of history is, this sermon does mark a dangerous escalation in the rhetoric coming from the Moscow Patriarchate – and, we can assume, by extension the Russian state. This rhetorical advance is made all the more dangerous by the fact that most in the West won't even know the sermon happened, let alone be aware of its pernicious implications.

It is understandable why. Patriarch Kirill is not deploying the familiar rhetoric of the Culture Wars, 'gay pride parades' and Western decadence, he is speaking in terms of the obscure history of the Christian East, a history largely unknown in the West. But do not be fooled; what he is saying is extremely dangerous.

Patriarch Kirill's sermon on the Sunday of St John Climacus does no less than refuse to acknowledge the distinction between Russian and Ukrainian culture and identity, and it denies Ukraine's right to exist as a sovereign nation, both historically and in the present. Furthermore, it legitimizes the ongoing violence as necessary and even, perhaps one could argue, holy.

As the Patriarch says, recalling the words of the Gospel of John, the Russian soldiers are 'laying down their lives for a friend'. That is right. The Ukrainians the Russians are bombing, shooting and leaving dead at the side of the road are friends, friends in the manner that Jesus thought of his disciples. These are the words of a committed nationalist of the imperial variety and a man who thinks nothing of using the familiar words of faith to their most egregious effect. As we should all know by now, this is a very dangerous combination. When we ignore his words (and when we are too generous in our interpretation of them), we betray those he has already harmed and we virtually ensure that he will do worse in the future.

April 12, 2022

Meet 'The Putin Whisperer': Kirill may lead the Russian Church, but this Metropolitan has Putin's ear

Patriarch Kirill, the head of the Russian Orthodox Church, is rightly getting the most attention with regards to the Russian Orthodox Church's unfailing (and unnerving) support for the invasion of Ukraine. The rouble stops with the boss. But there is another cleric who has perhaps even more influence over the Russian President than the Patriarch: the man rumoured to be Putin's personal confessor, Metropolitan Tikhon (Shevkunov). Although Metropolitan Tikhon has tacitly denied these rumours, there is a reason they have persisted and there is little doubt he has Putin's ear. So, who is he?

A committed nationalist and a reactionary among reactionaries, Metropolitan Tikhon is a man simultaneously haunted by the ghosts of the past and enchanted by the temptations of our age. Understanding this politically savvy monk is critical to understanding Putin, his war on Ukraine and the role of religion in shaping both.

Born Georgiy Alexandrovich Shevkunov in Moscow during the days of Nikita Khrushchev, the man who would become one of Russia's most powerful bishops, first aimed to be a filmmaker. In 1982, the same year he graduated from film school, he was baptized and entered the famed Holy Dormition Pskovo-Pechersky Monastery shortly after. At the time, the elder of the monastery was Archimandrite John (Krestyankin), one of the most revered clerics of the Soviet era, having spent five years in prison camps after refusing to co-operate with the Communist regime.

I say this to ward off any accusations that Metropolitan Tikhon is not sufficiently 'Orthodox' or even 'Christian'. He is very much both, a man whose life and career place him at the centre of the Orthodox tradition and the contemporary history of Orthodox Christianity in Russia. While certainly not representative of the entirety of an ancient and complex community he is, nonetheless, indisputably part of it.

That being said, unlike his famous spiritual father, when it comes to Metropolitan Tikhon, rumours of collaboration with the Soviet regime have long swirled around the slightly too-polished monk. Even before joining the Church, in his student days as a Leninist Komsomol activist, he earned the nickname 'Sheptunov' (the whistleblower), based on the suspicion that he was working with the KGB.

Later, in the last days of the Soviet Union, Metropolitan Tikhon, by then a monk, began working at the publishing office for the Moscow Patriarchate. His colleagues there say that they began to receive visits from KGB agents. Tellingly, some rumours suggest that Tikhon defended his collaboration as necessary to prevent 'Satanists and Islamists' from overrunning the country.

After the fall of Communism, when a liberal faction in the Russian Orthodox Church sought to start celebrating services in modern Russian (as opposed to Old Church Slavonic), Tikhon led the reaction against them. Father Georgy Kochetkov, one of the advocates for modern Russian, saw his church targeted by vigilantes and was ultimately forbidden from serving as a priest for three years. It is widely understood that attacks on Father Kochetkov were committed at the direction of Tikhon – episodes one cannot help but recall when thinking about recent events at St Nicholas Orthodox Church in Amsterdam, where opposition to the reactionary position was met with vandalism and threats.

From these events in the last years of the USSR and the first of the Russian Federation, we can learn much about who the Metropolitan is as a man and a priest. More than just a conservative or a reactionary, he is a man willing to use any means at his disposal to ward off what he sees as the forces of evil. It would seem that, for him, there is no institution so corrupt, no method too violent as to forgo its use if it means keeping out 'the Satanists and the Islamists', which essentially includes any outside force opposed to Tikhon's harsh and austere version of Orthodox Christianity.

While Archimandrite John (Krestyankin) risked the Soviet gulag rather than collaborate with the Communists, his protégé Tikhon has seen no harm in collaboration with the secular powers. There is a strange symmetry here with Patriarch Kirill, whose grandfather, Father Vasily Gundyaev, spent time in a re-education camp for his struggle against Russian Orthodox collaboration with the Soviets. He also, as evidenced by his attack on Father Kochetkov, clearly does not oppose violence directed at other Orthodox Christians, if the reason is 'right'.

Throughout his clerical career, Metropolitan Tikhon has maintained a robust creative life – one that provides us insight into what he might be thinking. (You can even visit his website if you're so inclined.) Perhaps most important for our purposes is his 2008 film *The Death of An Empire: Byzantine Lessons.* The film's central thesis is that a geographically large and demographically diverse state (such as the Byzantine Empire was and Russia is) must be governed by a strong (perhaps even totalitarian) government, or it risks being pulled apart by conflicts from within and opportunistic enemies from without.

To Metropolitan Tikhon, the latter, in the case of the Byzantines, seems to him to be composed primarily of prospecting

Jews and jealous Western European nations. The message is clear: Russia, the heir of the Byzantine Empire, must learn from her collapse, maintaining the power of the state and cultivating suspicion of hostile outsiders.

The Death of Empire is not merely an articulation of the Russia World ideology (although it certainly plays with its most fundamental concerns). Importantly, the film downplays nationalist ambitions in their strictest sense, focusing on religion rather than national identity as the principal source of unity in a state. The film is a treatise on how not only Russia, but the whole of the Eastern Christian world, ought to understand itself, from its most traumatic losses to its most glorious triumphs.

A world brimming with divine grace

But Metropolitan Tikhon is also the author of *Everyday Saints and Other Stories*, a collection that one advertisement calls 'an insider's look at a Russian Orthodox monastery'. Part hagiography and part spiritual memoir, with a sprinkling of political manifesto, the book is important due to its popularity: it has sold well over three million copies in Russia and has been translated into at least 17 languages. It has also won several national book awards and been at the centre of diplomatic receptions. In other words, this is a very popular book.

Everyday Saints is infused with the mysticism that seems to entice so many to Christianity's Eastern expression. It is also a book filled with a rigid and distinct morality. And yet at the same time, it is a beautiful book and right at home in a tradition whose hagiographic literature holds almost the same authority as Scripture (and, if we are being honest, in practice frequently holds more). There is a compassion and pragmatism contained within this anthology of lives and memories that reminds me why I remain a member of this complicated faith.

But *Everyday Saints* is also a stark reminder – at least it should be – of how complicated the religious dimension of this current conflict truly is. Written by a man to whom, rumour has it, Vladimir Putin whispers his sins, a man from whom the Russian president seeks spiritual counsel, the book presents a complex picture, one that is difficult for Western eyes to comprehend and yet has proven strangely appealing time and time again.

As someone from 'the other side' of the internal conflict within Orthodoxy, I find in *Everyday Saints* a familiarity that frankly I cannot see in his other works, such as *The Death of Empire*, and that familiarity frightens me. It is easy to denounce everything coming from Vladimir Putin and his spiritual accomplices as heresy (and a great deal of it to my mind is just that), but we must also recognize the ways in which their ugliness is the product of the same heritage that has also produced so much beauty.

It is also good to remember that Tikhon and Kirill (and Putin for that matter) are all men of a very particular era – Soviet men – raised in the official atheism of the USSR. These are men who spent their childhoods in a system that told them that, by human effort and human progress, the world could be made new and better. And then they found, like all their comrades, that the promised new world was a lie. After that, how would they not be suspicious of the Siren song of 'progress'? They watched as fathers, both spiritual and physical, suffered at the hands of the Soviet regime, vainly trying to keep Orthodoxy pure (whatever that means). How would they not be obsessed with its purity now?

Unlike Kirill, who was raised in the faith, Tikhon came to religion as a young man. He writes in *Everyday Saints* about the refuge he found there, his horror at the outside world with its evil and corruption. How could this experience not leave him ready to do anything to defend his refuge from that evil he had just barely escaped?

Like Kirill, he became a priest in the Soviet era and instead of choosing the path of resistance and suffering, they chose collaboration and saw the USSR collapse and the Church reborn at the centre of Russian power. Did they take this accident of history to mean they had done the right thing?

I do not write this to excuse the evil both men have encouraged and allowed. I write this because I am conscious of the words of the great Russian writer and anti-Communist dissenter, Aleksandr Solzhenitsyn, who wrote: 'The line dividing good and evil cuts through the heart of every human being. And who is willing to destroy a piece of his own heart?'

The Orthodox faith I share with these men whose actions I cannot comprehend teaches me that there is real evil in the world, but human beings, made as they are in the image of God, are not evil. Concepts like 'total depravity' and 'original sin' are not part of the Orthodox consciousness. Human beings might be marred by evil deeds and words, but the image of the good God lies underneath, indestructible. It is a difficult thing to believe these days, but I try. Not least because I want to understand who these men, including Metropolitan Tikhon, are, even if their actions leave me utterly horrified and thoroughly confused.

I am left only with the lines of a hymn, sung on Great and Holy Thursday (Maundy Thursday, in the Western practice) at a service commemorating Christ's betrayal by Judas, one of his chosen disciples:

> Behold, O lover of money (*and one could substitute here, power, prestige, religion, family – anything save God*), the man who for love of money hangs himself.
>
> Flee, O my soul, from the greed that would dare such things against the Master.

May 9, 2022

How belief in Moscow as the 'New Rome' explains Kirill's astonishing declaration that 'Russia has never attacked anyone'

Saying outrageous, verifiably untrue things has sort of become Patriarch Kirill of Moscow's brand. Increasingly, his rhetoric has turned to the idea that Ukraine is not actually a sovereign nation, but simply a part of Russia. Last Tuesday, he took this claim to the next level. Gone were the veiled references; instead, in a sermon at the Kremlin's Archangel Cathedral, the Patriarch of Moscow declared: 'Russia has never attacked anyone. It is amazing that a great and powerful country has not attacked anyone, it only defended its borders.'

What's clear is that Kirill does not see this as a lie easily caught by any child with a map, but instead thinks it is the map that is lying. Ukraine does not exist and thus Russian military action in Ukraine is Russian military action to defend its borders.

This is not just a political supposition but a theological one, underwritten by Moscow's centuries-long claim to be 'the Third Rome. Not only is this belief powerful in Russia, but it helps simultaneously to foster both pro-Russian sympathy and to elicit anti-Russian fear in other parts of the Orthodox world. It is also a self-conception that Russia shares with many Christians, especially in America, whether these Christians are aware of it or not.

The continuous succession and perpetual survival of the Roman Empire is an important concept that runs throughout the whole of European and Eastern Mediterranean history, a testament not only to the power and prestige of the Roman Empire but to the religious significance attached to the Empire after its conversion to Christianity. In this conception, the Roman Empire had existed by divine will to facilitate the spread of the Christian faith; it had been baptized and had in turn baptized the world.

This divine mission made the Empire's collapse theologically problematic – thus claims to be the inheritor of the Roman legacy were always less about political prestige (although that has certainly played a part) than about carrying on the divine destiny of a baptized Rome.

Moscow has been the most persistent modern claimant to the Roman legacy in the Christian East. Even before the fall of Constantinople in 1453, Rus princes, like Boris of Tver, were beginning to play with the notion that they were heirs to the Roman legacy. These efforts were only amplified after the Byzantine Empire fell at last to the Ottomans. With Constantinople – a.k.a. 'the New Rome' – now in the hands of Muslim rulers and the West in the grip of perceived papal heresy, Moscow and her Grand Princes increasingly sought to place themselves in the role of successor to the Empire.

Part of this claim involved a tradition of predictions and prophecies declaring that Russia would ultimately liberate Constantinople (modern-day Istanbul) and return it to Christian rule. The earliest written evidence of this idea comes from Nestor Iskander's *Tale on the Taking of Tsargrad*, which dates from the late fifteenth or early sixteenth century (and thus very close to the actual fall of Constantinople). It is a prophecy that has been frequently repeated, including most famously in recent history by St Paisios of Mount Athos, an influential late-twentieth-century Greek cleric.

The liberation of Constantinople has taken on further significance. No longer merely a single political or military act, for some the reclamation of Constantinople signifies a much broader type of liberation, a near-cosmic event which will see Orthodoxy triumph over a sinful world. Thus Russia, in this view, is not just a military power on the side of the Orthodox Faith but is (like the baptized Rome) a divinely chosen baptizing, Christianizing agent in an immoral world.

For example, since the Russian invasion of Ukraine, the controversial Cypriot bishop Metropolitan Neophytos of Morphou (probably most famous in the West for claiming that women who enjoy anal sex have gay children) declared his support for the Russian invasion as a necessary purging of the Earth on account of the fact that we live in an age with 'a lot of sin, a lot of disrespect and a lot of infidelity'. He has importantly reiterated the liberator role of Russia, as prophesied by Elder Paisios.

He has made subsequent statements, including a claim that the Virgin Mary has appeared to inform 'a pious man' that the war in Ukraine has been allowed by God to continue because of unrepented sexual immorality and abortion. Russia is, in this paradigm, rebaptizing Ukraine and bringing it back into the fold of a holy Roman Empire. Furthermore, Ukraine is within the borders of Russia, because, as a contemporary Rome, the world is its border.

While this idea is apparently comforting to some in the Orthodox world, it is extremely disconcerting to others. For example, from where I sit in Iasi, Romania, the old capital near the Romanian–Moldovan border, the idea of a Russia with borders ordained by God is a very disconcerting notion.

To be clear, both Romania and Moldova remain deeply conservative and unquestionably religious nations. But they are also countries, particularly Romania, that over the past two decades have increasingly looked westward. Romania is a member of the European Union and NATO. It held the European Council presidency in 2019, a fact still celebrated in Bucharest airport.

If anything, for these western-facing Romanians, like their Greek counterparts, the new Rome is not Moscow but Brussels. Russian claims that the borders of nation states – most of which are notably less than 200 years old – do not have any significance, are dangerous claims for these kinds of Orthodox nations and people that are looking to modernize, and, ultimately, to Westernize.

Western Christians, particularly American Protestant ones, often scoff at the succession of Romes that still capture the imagination of Eastern Christians. But American white Evangelicals and other parts of the Christian Right are not far from holding these same ideas about America, even if they do not tend to identify it as such. Most obviously, the Latter-day Saint movement traditionally views America as the site of the Garden of Eden and the future New Jerusalem, a new Holy Land.

Just as early Christians believed Rome existed to facilitate the spread of the Christian Gospel, many Mormons today believe the USA exists to facilitate the Restoration. Furthermore, many American Evangelicals believe American exceptionalism derives from the fact that America has been given a special mission from God. In addition to describing 'Christian Nationalism', these are both ways of saying America is the new Rome for people whose religious sympathies are not quite as enthusiastic about Late Antique and Medieval Christianity as the Orthodox and Catholics.

And this similarity should serve as a warning. Patriarch Kirill believes that borders do not, ultimately, matter because Russia has a global mission. Some Americans believe the same. Both want to be Rome, whether they say it or not. And for a world on the brink, that is very bad news.

May 19, 2022

Putin's theo-propaganda minister invokes 600 years of history to lay claim to Ukraine

In 17 May, Patriarch Kirill of Moscow addressed the upper house of the Russian Parliament in a speech that highlighted the role of the Russian Orthodox Church and its primate as a propaganda agent par excellence for the Putin regime. It also demonstrated, once again, the extent to which the Russian state and the Russian Orthodox Church rely upon a version of history that is utterly foreign to most in the West, and yet is utterly common in the Orthodox Christian world, even beyond Russia. Unfortunately, Western media have all but ignored this element of Russian propaganda, in no small part because the history itself is so foreign to its audience. They (understandably) want to report the news, not give a lecture in Eastern European history.

At the same time, this oversight speaks to a larger problem in how we report on and discuss the role of history in current events, particularly as it relates to religion. The Abrahamic religions, in particular, are deeply invested in their historical narratives. The God of Judaism, Christianity and Islam is a god of history, a god who intervenes in human events and seeks to mould the narrative of history to a particular end. History, therefore, becomes a sacred narrative for these faiths. Consequently, challenging a faith's traditional version of history in this context is akin to challenging the faith itself. And we know how the media feel about that.

During the speech, Kirill focused on the idea that '. . . the people of Russia and Ukraine, who emerged from the common Kyiv Baptismal font, are united by the Orthodox faith and bound by a common historical destiny . . .'.

Furthermore, he recalled specific events from the past nearly 600 years that are widely known in the Orthodox Christian world, and particularly in Russia, to signify the West's attempts to undermine the political power of Orthodox states and to (worse yet) subsume Orthodoxy into the Christian West: the Union of Brest in 1596 and the eighteenth-century betrayal of Ivan Mazepa. (Before I explain both, raise your hand, dear reader, if you've heard of either . . . That's what I thought).

First the Union of Brest: in 1588, the Patriarch of Constantinople, Jeremias II, travelled to the Polish–Lithuanian Commonwealth and the Grand Duchy of Moscow and formally acknowledged the Russian Orthodox Church, which had claimed its own independence in 1458, in the wake of the fall of the Byzantine Empire to the Ottomans. This event is very important for contemporary Russian claims to Ukraine. After all, Kyiv, not Moscow, is the birthplace of Slavic Orthodoxy.

The chief bishop of the Slavs moved from Kyiv to Moscow for political, not theological, reasons. Without Jeremias's trip, the historical claim of Moscow's authority over the Ukrainian Church disappears. In fact, without Jeremias's trip, the argument could easily run in the other direction: i.e. that Moscow should be under the authority of Kyiv. Jeremias also deposed the existing metropolitan bishop of Kyiv and replaced him with a more friendly metropolitan.

Well, it turns out the idea of Moscow as the centre of secular and religious power in Eastern Europe was just as controversial in the sixteenth century as in the twenty-first. After Jeremias left, nine out of the ten local bishops in the affected regions gathered in Brest and voted to join the Roman Catholic Church. The Greek Catholic Church is a product of this event.

Patriarch Kirill also mentioned Ivan Mazepa's 'betrayal' to an audience that effectively constitutes the Russian senate. A Ruthenian-Lithuanian noble man born around 50 years after the Union of Brest, Mazepa was by all accounts well educated and cosmopolitan. He spent a great deal of time in Western Europe and even served as a courtier to the Polish king, experiences that would make the Russian state suspect him of being potentially 'Catholized'.

Nonetheless, in 1687, he was made Hetman (essentially a general) of the Zaporizhian Host in what is now Ukraine. In 1708, in the midst of the Great Northern War, upon learning that he was going to be deposed as Hetman by the Tsar, Mazepa deserted his army and joined the forces of King Charles XII of Sweden.

A Russian victory at the Battle of Poltava meant that Mazepa's intention of bringing Ukraine into Swedish possession would never be realized, but the consequences of his changing sides have reverberated throughout Ukrainian and Russian history. Kirill's claim that Mazepa has been recently rehabilitated in Ukraine is nothing short of accusing the current Ukrainian government of a similar betrayal, not just of Russia, but of Orthodoxy itself. After all, Mazepa's name was (until 1869) one of those read alongside other anathematized people and ideas during the Sunday of Orthodoxy, the first Sunday of Lent. The message is clear: to betray Russia is to betray the Orthodox Faith, perhaps even to betray Christ himself.

To be clear, Kirill is not wrong that Ukrainians are more divided on Mazepa's legacy. Polling shows that about a third of Ukrainians see him as a 'man who fought for Ukraine's independence', while nearly a quarter see him as a traitor. And the former president of Ukraine, Viktor Yushchenko, would not rule out the idea that his family was connected to the former Hetman. He even had a statue of him built in the middle of Kyiv.

But that's kind of the point. History is not just a series of things that happened. History is what we think those events mean. Our interpretations usually have everything to do with the present and very little to do with the past. To see this, one need look no further than America's own contentious political debate about how its racial history ought to be taught.[1] Is the story of American race-based chattel slavery one of a glorious triumph over racism and oppression, and thus proof of American exceptionalism? Or is it a story of continuing prejudice and violence that reveals not only that American exceptionalism is a lie but that America is a fundamentally racist society? Clearly, this is a question that has much more to do with our century than that of Abraham Lincoln.

This is also, to be clear, a religious question. For many American Christians, particularly some American evangelicals and members of the Latter-day Saint movement, American history is as sacred and theologically charged as medieval and early modern Eastern Mediterranean and Eastern European history is for Orthodox Christians. If you believe in a god of history, you inevitably also believe your own history is divinely mandated and so look to it for proof of your own righteousness.

Patriarch Kirill is not doing anything different from his friend Franklin Graham – and both men clearly understand that the history of their respective nations is a Christian one, ordained by God. This is a dangerous way of thinking, but it is all the more dangerous if we do not know what they are even talking about. Which is why history is always worth knowing.

1 This is in no way intended to suggest that both are legitimate, ethical and equally supported by professional historians – just that they demonstrate how dramatically opposed interpretations of history can be.

September 23, 2022

Now Kirill justifies Russia's invasion as a defence of Orthodox faith

If you have been educated in North America or Western Europe, you might be forgiven for having never heard of the Battle of Kulikovo, a battle between Russian forces and the Golden Horde, on 8 September 1380, in which the Russian forces emerged victorious. Although Mongol domination of what is today Russia did not end that day, the victory at Kulikovo is roughly regarded as the beginning of the end of the Mongol occupation and the birth of modern Russia. The eighth of September is also the date on which Orthodox Christians (along with Catholics and some Anglicans) commemorate the birth of the Virgin Mary. The coincidence of these two dates has been an important touchstone in Russian self-understanding.

The Russian Orthodox Church still uses the so-called 'Old Calendar', according to which this past Wednesday (21 September) was 8 September. The celebration of this major holiday occurred the day after Russian President Vladimir Putin announced his 'partial mobilization' of some 300,000 Russian reservists, a clear response to the string of defeats Russia has suffered in Ukraine in recent weeks.

Patriarch Kirill of Moscow, the head of the Russian Orthodox Church, consequently used the celebration of the feast to demonstrate once again that he is fully prepared to act as Putin's religious propaganda machine. While celebrating the Divine Liturgy on Wednesday at the Zachatyevsky Monastery, which is traditionally considered the oldest convent in Moscow (a historically dubious claim), the Patriarch began his sermon by recalling, not the birth of the Holy Mother, but the birth of the Fatherland at the Battle of Kulikovo.

'Today is significant in the history of our Fatherland for many reasons, but perhaps the most striking and significant is the Battle of Kulikovo', he tells the gathered faithful, before noting that the enemy had not known that the Russians' prayers were likely more effective on a day dedicated to the Virgin Mary, implying that the Russian victory that day had been a direct result of the interventions of the Holy Mother.

Not that the woman whom Orthodox Christians widely refer to as the Theotokos (the God-bearer) – i.e. the Virgin Mary, whose birth is the cause of the feast day – gets much attention during the rest of the oration. Because she doesn't. Instead, Patriarch Kirill remains much more focused on the famed battle and its lessons for his contemporary flock. He declares that, while retreat might be possible from worldly things, it is impossible to retreat 'from faith', a powerful line, now a standard in his sermons, which draws an equivalency between Russian aggression in Ukraine and defending and living the Orthodox faith.

He then goes on to, once again, erase Ukraine from the historical map, saying that the people ought to pray that 'Holy Russia would be reunited'. As he has made clear before, Ukraine is not, to his mind, an independent nation, but a rogue territory within Russia. And keeping Ukraine as part of Russia is a sacred obligation. It is also apparently what victory looks like for the Virgin Mary (she does get a look in at the end).

It is easy, after all these months, to stop listening to the ramblings of a far-off cleric who is clearly in the pocket of a dangerous authoritarian who has his finger on a nuclear button.

Clearly, it is not good for one's peace of mind. Add to that his insistence on referencing a history that is completely obscure in the West.

However, Patriarch Kirill is sending a clear message about how he sees the war in Ukraine and how he and Vladimir Putin would like the Russian people to see it. If we stop paying attention, we do so at our peril.

Part 3

THIS IS NOT JUST A PROBLEM FOR UKRAINE

December 12, 2018

Russians on la rue Daru

At 12 rue Daru in Paris's 8th arrondissement stands the Cathédrale Saint-Alexandre-Nevsky. There, on the right bank of the Seine, within walking distance of the Arc de Triomphe and Elysée Palace, Saint-Alexandre-Nevsky's onion-shaped domes and vaulted stone arches seem both utterly foreign and entirely native pressed against the Parisian skyline. Built in the middle of the nineteenth century with a donation from Tsar Alexander II and consecrated in 1861, this is the oldest existing Russian Orthodox house of worship in France. And since the Russian Revolution in 1917, the cathedral has served as the headquarters of one of the most vibrant, fascinating and unique factions of the complex (and frequently quite literally Byzantine) Orthodox Christian world: Patriarchal Exarchate for Orthodox Parishes of the Russian Tradition in Western Europe.

Today, the Cathédrale Saint-Alexandre-Nevsky stands at the centre of a community crisis. It is, without doubt, a small community. The entire jurisdiction consists of only 100 parishes, two monasteries, seven sketes (a uniquely Eastern Christian monastic community that is essentially a collection of hermits) and one very famous theological school. But it has found itself caught in the middle of a growing dispute between the Patriarchates of Constantinople and Moscow. It is a conflict that could be (and has been at different points in history) merely a parochial skirmish between two hierarchs from some of the most embattled, albeit ancient, corners of the Christian world. But this is far from the case today. With Vladimir Putin in the

Kremlin, the Russian Orthodox Church has resumed its position at the heart of Russian political life. And the Moscow-based Church increasingly serves as an instrument of Russian soft power, including in places such as Ukraine, where the oversight of Orthodox parishes in the country has become a proxy pitched battle in the country's large issues with Russian intervention.

In fact, the conflict in Ukraine is the immediate cause for the Exarchate's current troubles, although its history begins in the upheaval of the Russian Revolution. While there had been a small Russian expatriate community in France since the early modern period, it was not until the Russian Revolution that large numbers of Russians began to stream into France. Of the nearly 1.5 million refugees who fled in the wake of the Revolution and subsequent civil war, approximately 400,000 found their way to France. There, these exiles faced a serious battle in preserving their religious traditions during the diaspora. While Orthodox immigrant communities in the West had ordinarily 'sent home' for priests, thus maintaining the cultural and jurisdictional ties that bound them to their traditional apostolic sees, the Russians arriving in France had little reason to seek to nurture such a relationship with the Patriarchate of Moscow, which had at this point largely been co-opted by the new Communist government. The obvious alternative choice was the Russian Orthodox Church Outside of Russia (ROCOR), a sort of Church-in-exile that had been set up in the wake of the events of 1917 and 1918. Metropolitan Eulogius, the spiritual head of the Russian Orthodox in France, had been one of its founding members after all. However, by the early 1930s, tensions within ROCOR, as well as questions about its legitimacy, compelled Metropolitan Eulogius to seek the 'canonical protection' of Patriarch Photius II of Constantinople. The Greek Patriarch received the embattled Russian bishop and one of the most peculiar outposts of the Orthodox Christian world was born: a small collection of parishes and monasteries exiled primarily in France observing Russian cultural and religious customs under the protection of the Greek Patriarch, himself a kind of internal exile in Turkey.

And yet, this strange little band of castaways proved to be one of the greatest sources of intellectual light in the rather dark world of modern Orthodoxy. Just eight years after the Russian Revolution that had sent them into the wilderness, in 1925, the emigrés founded St Sergius Orthodox Theological Institute. The list of the school's former teachers and students reads like a 'Who's Who of Modern Orthodox Theology': Nicolas Afanassieff, Élisabeth Behr-Sigel, Olivier Clément, Georges Florovsky, Nicolas Lossky, John Meyendorff and Alexandre Schmemann. While largely unknown to those uninterested in theology or Eastern Christianity, the simple fact is that it is no stretch to argue that every truly great Orthodox Christian thinker of the twentieth century has passed through St Sergius's doors. Importantly, the intellectual vibrancy of the school created what is perhaps the only modern progressive threads in Orthodox Christian theology. While certainly much of this (including, for example, treatises arguing for the restoration of women to the diaconate) would hardly pass as liberal or progressive among most Western mainline Protestants or even Roman Catholics, for the Orthodox world much of what has been produced there is nothing short of revolutionary. This kind of cutting-edge scholarship could, in part, only exist because of the unique nature of the Exarchate, a band of exiles, largely left to their own devices, living and working in Western Europe throughout the changes of the twentieth century. It was a reality that made the Exarchate both valuable and dangerous.

The Moscow Patriarchate and the Russian Orthodox Church began their comeback almost immediately after the collapse of the Soviet Union. But this progress was sluggish at first and it was unclear what role the Russian Orthodox Church would play in Russia, let alone the rest of the world. However, there is no doubt that things have changed. On 1 February 2009, the St Petersburg-born Vladimir Mikhailovich Gundyayev was enthroned as Kirill I, Patriarch of Moscow and All the Rus. Kirill has nurtured a close relationship with Vladimir Putin as well as leaders of the American Right such as Franklin Graham. Under his leadership, the Russian Orthodox Church has become a voice for social conservatism, not just in Russia but around the world, attracting far-right activists in Europe and American Evangelicals into its sphere of influence. In this capacity, it has challenged the authority and influence of the Ecumenical Patriarchate of Constantinople and its current incumbent Bartholomew I, who is generally seen as more progressive.

Their growing conflict has played out in Ukraine, where Bartholomew has granted freedom from Moscow's control to the Ukrainian Orthodox, a move that has met with predictable opposition from Moscow and has brought the Orthodox world closer to schism than any other event for hundreds of years. This is where the Exarchate comes in.

Since the collapse of Communism in Russia, and certainly since the Moscow Patriarchate united with ROCOR in 2007, Moscow has had its eye on its lost children in Western Europe. As the conflict in Ukraine heated up, the Patriarch of Constantinople played one of his most underrated cards. In late 2018, he dissolved the Patriarchal Exarchate for Orthodox Parishes of the Russian Tradition in Western Europe, ordering that the parishes, monasteries and theological schools all come under the authority of a Greek bishop. In essence, erasing the Russian-ness of a community that had existed largely to preserve this identity. Within a month, Moscow announced it was creating its own Exarchate, a Russian exarchate, with no Greek bishops to meddle in their traditions.

Few doubt that the Exarchate is being offered up in exchange for the wealthier and more numerous churches of Ukraine, and it has left the people of the Exarchate with a nearly impossible choice. The reality is that, whether the Exarchate is absorbed into the Greek dominions of Western Europe or whether it comes under Moscow, the Exarchate as is will cease to exist. It will lose either its Russian identity to the powerful influence of Greek diaspora cultural preservation (forces with which anyone who has seen *My Big Fat Greek Wedding* will be familiar), or it will lose its intellectual vibrancy, its culture of free inquiry, to the oversight of an increasingly reactionary Russian Orthodox Church. Another option is for the Exarchate to vote to preserve itself as independent of either Patriarch. This would make it 'non-canonical', a technical term for any Orthodox jurisdiction not in communion with other Orthodox churches, but also a status that brings with it a lack of credibility within Orthodoxy that would inevitably undermine the Exarchate's tradition of influence.

In short, there are no good ways out. One of the Orthodox world's brightest lights, one of its few hopes for a modern faith, is being snuffed out for short-term gain. And this should concern everyone, whether or not they have any vested interest in the Eastern Christian tradition. The Russian Orthodox Church, acting in no small part as an agent of the Putin regime, has been increasingly successful in deploying its narrow, reactionary and reductive version of Orthodox Christianity as an important tool on the international stage, positioning itself and, by extension, Putin's Russia as guardians of 'traditional Christian society'. The best Orthodox defences against that dangerous philosophy have been nurtured in the Exarchate and at St Sergius. To lose this community now would be to lose this precious counterbalance. It is a loss all of us can ill afford.

January 21, 2022

Russian influence in sub-Saharan Africa and the lessons of Ukraine

Russian aggression in Ukraine has been in the news lately and the threat of a full-scale Russian invasion of that borderland nation and the inevitable response from NATO constitutes perhaps the most dangerous geopolitical situation of our day. But this is not a contemporary problem. Russia has had its eyes on Ukraine for centuries and exercising religious control has been part of that.

That is why, when the Patriarch of Constantinople (theoretically 'the first among equals' among Orthodox bishops) granted the Ukrainian Orthodox Church full autonomy from the Russian Orthodox Church in October 2018, a status known as 'autocephaly', the reaction from Moscow's secular and ecclesiastical authorities was strong and swift. In fact, the fallout from that 2018 decision has continued to divide the Orthodox world and talks of a full split between Moscow and Constantinople are in the air.

Most recently, the battle has moved to Africa. On 29 December 2021, the Holy Synod of the Moscow Patriarchate, the leading body of the Russian Orthodox Church, announced its decision to establish a Patriarchal exarchate in Africa. Exarchates descend from Byzantine administrative districts and have functioned as a way for Orthodox bishops to set up zones of influence in geographical areas outside their prescribed regions. In modern practice, exarchates are, among other things, a way of getting behind enemy lines to establish spheres of influence where one does not necessarily belong. The new Russian exarchate in Africa is expected to include 102 clerics in eight African countries. All of the clerics, newly under the patronage of Moscow, were formerly members of the Greek Orthodox Patriarchate of Alexandria and the Moscow Synod is explicitly tying its decision to create the new exarchate and welcome these clergy to the Patriarch of Alexandria's decision to acknowledge the independence of the Ukrainian Church.

And so an ecclesiastical conflict born from one geopolitical turf war has moved to another site of the New Great Game. Modern Russia also has designs on Africa, where it seeks to compete with China and the Western powers for influence in a continent of natural resources and growing markets. Furthermore, there is little doubt that Russia has, in recent years, sought increasingly to use the Russian Orthodox Church as an instrument of foreign influence: in Ukraine, Serbia, Western Europe and the USA. It is foolish to think that Africa would be any different. Maybe there are 102 African clerics so angry about the independence of the Ukrainian Church that they are aligning themselves with Moscow. Maybe this decision is purely about church governance, happening completely in a vacuum. But that, considering everything else, seems a bit absurd.

The Orthodox Church in Africa is neither wealthy nor large. With the exception of some significant Greek communities in Egypt and South Africa (who are decidedly not in the market for a new Russian bishop), the relatively few African convert communities on the continent are neither financially affluent nor politically powerful – yet. By staking a claim to these communities, these growing communities, the Russian Orthodox Church and, by extension, its friends in the Kremlin, are further seeking to exert their political, cultural and ultimately economic influence in Africa. Something that the ties of this conflict to Ukraine make clear.

Both Africa and Orthodoxy tend to be ignored in the West, so it is easy to understand how a story about them both has missed media attention. But this is a story we ignore at our own peril. Africa, with its natural resources and rapidly expanding population, will inevitably play a significant role in the coming decades. Influence on the continent will be even more valuable than it is today. Moscow is setting the stage to expand its African power, cultural and otherwise. And we should be paying attention. We might be looking at the next Ukraine.

Note: As of February 2023. The Patriarchal Exarchate of Africa has representatives in nineteen African countries.

February 24, 2022

The enigmatic role of antisemitism in the Russia–Ukraine conflict

As noted recently in the *New York Times* and elsewhere, the Jews of Ukraine have plenty of cause for concern. History has not been kind to the Jewish communities of Eastern Europe: from pogroms to the Holocaust, the memory of historical trauma is very much alive. But as Russia pursues its war in Ukraine, history is not the only reason for Ukraine's Jewish community to be afraid.

A not-so-latent antisemitism lies at the heart of Putin's propaganda machine and appeals to antisemitic sentiments have been a central theme in the kultur politick advanced by both Russia and the Russian Orthodox Church in the Putin era. For example, whatever sympathy Russia does get from the West relies in no small part on shared antisemitism and a perception that Russia (and frequently Russian Orthodoxy) is essentially anti-Jewish. This strategy has been on full display with respect to Ukraine. To be clear, there is a certain irony to this, since Putin's government and Kirill's patriarchate have arguably been some of the least openly antisemitic in Russian history (notably a very low bar), a fact underscored by the support Putin enjoys among Russian Jews.

That being said, there is one particular Jewish person that Putin and his regime clearly hate: Ukrainian President Volodymyr Zelenskyy. And there is apparently no concern about allowing antisemitic tropes to govern their treatment of him. For example, in October of last year, Deputy Chairman of the

Security Council (and former president) Dmitry Medvedev published a shocking, expletive-filled attack on Ukraine and its president.

In addition to repeating the Putin regime's persistent claim that Ukraine has no distinct cultural identity and that Moscow is the sole and rightful heir of the Kyivan Rus, Medvedev referred to Zelenskyy as 'a man with certain ethnic roots' and suggested that Zelenskyy has concealed his Jewish identity to serve the interests of Ukrainian nationalists. Medvedev went even further and suggested that Zelenskyy's 'betrayal' of Russia made him akin to a Sonderkommando, Jewish prisoners in Nazi death camps forced to help dispose of those killed in the gas chambers.

But the threat is not just directed at Zelenskyy. This week US officials sent a letter to the UN High Commissioner for Human Rights revealing that, according to credible US intelligence, Russian forces in the disputed regions intended to target Russian and Belorussian dissidents living in Ukraine, including religious and ethnic minorities, journalists and LGBT activists. And state-controlled Russian media continue to push theories alleging that the Ukrainian government meddled in the 2016 US election at the direction of George Soros (a theory that may very well be shared by Rudy Giuliani), who often figures prominently in antisemitic conspiracy theories, both in the USA and elsewhere.

What is truly fascinating about the entire thing is that the Kremlin has gone out of its way to make its recent not-so-terrible track record with Jews a central part of its propaganda against Ukraine, a nation which, it has routinely asserted, is not some bastion of pro-Western sentiment but rather a regressive violator of human rights. Ukraine, according to Russian propaganda, is the structurally antisemitic country while Russia is just trying to help out the Jews of Ukraine.

Which brings us to the most realistic and imminent threat for Ukraine's Jewish community. There is a real danger that Russia will covertly perpetuate antisemitic violence, blame that violence on Ukrainian nationalists and then use it as pretext to commit further violence in the country. After all, Putin persists in claiming that his objective in the Ukraine is to 'de-Nazify' the country.

Eastern Europe's Jewish community is quite used to being used as pawns in the games of history. And as the next chapter in that complicated and often dark history commences, there is little reason to believe this time will be any different.

March 2, 2022

A twisted love story: how American Evangelicals helped make Putin's Russia, and how Russia became the darling of the American Right

If someone from 1965 were to arrive in a time machine, there is likely much about our current state of affairs that would shock them. But I cannot imagine anything that would be more confusing than the love affair between the American Right and Russia – the extent of which has come into stark clarity in the wake of Russia's invasion of Ukraine. Beyond Donald Trump's slightly unhinged, but wholly expected, comments praising Putin's 'genius' in illegally invading a sovereign nation, there are plenty of current 'mainstream' Republican elected officials who seem unclear as to whether Russian aggression on the front porch of NATO is a good idea or not.

How did this ever happen?

The answer, as with most things wrong with the contemporary GOP, lies in the party's almost complete takeover by evangelicals that began during the Nixon era.

Throughout the Cold War, the official atheism of Communist countries and the suppression of religion behind the Iron Curtain became a rallying cry for the American Right in general, and American evangelicals in particular, who made it their mission to save 'Godless Russia', seemingly unaware that, before 1917, it had, in fact, been 'Holy Mother Russia'.

In a pattern we've seen repeated again and again among American evangelicals before and since, they understood the Communist persecution of the local indigenous Christian population and the suppression of a region's historical Christian institutions to be primarily about themselves. And so, American evangelicals set about converting Russia to Christianity, a task that, with even a brief look at history, would have been revealed to have already been accomplished by the Byzantine Empire in the Middle Ages.

Almost immediately following the collapse of the Soviet Union, American evangelicals began to flood into Russia, with a generation coming of age on mission trips to Moscow and Bible-buying fundraisers for St Petersburg. Instead of meeting with hostility from the Russian Orthodox Church, these Protestant firebrands were generally welcomed. Which is the part of the story that is perhaps most difficult to explain; Orthodoxy as a faith tradition has spent centuries resolutely opposed to corruption or co-option from outside.

With a fear of foreign contamination that would put the most strident member of the Académie française to shame, Orthodox identity is resolutely grounded in notions of continuity and purity. Money and political influence are certainly part of the equation here, but there is another factor: on the other side of the Atlantic, the converts were flowing the other way.

The influx of Protestant American converts, many from the evangelical tradition but also conservative mainline Protestants, in the late 1980s and early 1990s radically changed the face of Orthodox Christianity in America. Once a Church almost exclusively made up of immigrants and their descendants, these Americans with no historical ties to Orthodoxy became a majority in a number of Orthodox jurisdictions in the USA and brought with them their cultural baggage – most importantly the Culture Wars.

The changes were obvious and immediate, both in traditional Orthodox countries and in the diaspora. Of course, Orthodoxy has never been gay affirming (despite John Boswell's eloquent but unsubstantiated claims) and abortion had been cause for excommunication since the Middle Ages, but the fact is no one really talked about those pet issues of the American Christian Right. Now Putin and Kirill unite around anti-LGBTQ laws, and Greek bishops make bizarre claims about why people are gay.

The creation of an Orthodox Christianity under the influence of American evangelical norms had real consequences, the rise of Orthodoxy as the new-found spiritual home of white nationalists being one of the more extreme. Among the less extreme consequences was that the rising number of conservative American Christians who identified as Orthodox started to soften opinions and change American right-wing perceptions of Russia.

Arguably, what this influx of American evangelicals into American Orthodox churches did was create a bridge over which American evangelicals in Russia were able to cross. An alliance began to take root which shaped Russia and the American Right as both headed into the twenty-first century.

Taking a page right out of the playbook of the Moral Majority, the Russian Orthodox Church has positioned itself as the leader of the conservative/traditionalist position, not only in Russia, but around the world. Putin's speech last Monday night made clear that Russia does not see itself as challenging the West and its values; rather, Putin's Russia is positioning itself as the last and rightful guardian of what the West once was and what it ought to be again: a Christian culture centred around family, faith and 'traditional values' that have been abandoned in the face of secular modernity.

Jerry Falwell's words have flown across time and space and landed in the mouth of a Russian president. Frequently referring to the 'so-called West', Putin lists the crimes of the NATO nations as including:

> They sought to destroy our traditional values and force on us their false values that would erode us, our people from within, the attitudes they have been aggressively imposing on their countries, attitudes that are directly leading to degradation and degeneration, because they are contrary to human nature. This is not going to happen.

The Russian Orthodox Church and the Russia of today are in no small part what American evangelicals have helped make it, from building literal churches to sending religious educational material, to guiding political policy. In return, both have found a powerful ally very close to the beating heart of American power. Today, as Ukrainian blood flows, some of that blood is on the hands of those American evangelicals who went off to convert a nation that was Christian before Europeans arrived in the Americas. Every mission trip and box of Bibles that arrived 'to Russia with love' helped to create this tragic moment.

March 30, 2022

Palestinian Orthodox Christians, desperate for help, have caught the attention of Russia

In case you are thinking that Ukraine is the only place in the world where Orthodox Christianity is embroiled in global conflict, please turn your eyes to Jerusalem. Two days ago, following an 18-year struggle, members of the Israeli settler organization, Ateret Cohanim, with the assistance of the police, took control of part of the Petra Hotel in the Christian Quarter of Jerusalem's Old City, drawing criticism from the city's Christian leaders, including the Greek Orthodox Patriarch of Jerusalem, who leads Israel's largest Christian community and whose church owns the seized hotel.

The vast majority of Christians in Israel are Palestinian Arabs, although they make up a small minority among Palestinians as a whole. Their status as a minority within a minority has been a source of significant difficulty for Arab Christians, and the sizable wealth of the Greek Orthodox Patriarchate of Jerusalem has made it a target for both the Israeli government and Palestinian Authority.

In 2020, an Israeli District Court ruled against the Patriarchate when it attempted to block the sale of other property to Ateret Cohanim. And Hamas has regularly targeted Palestinian Christians for discrimination, including attempting to curb the public celebration of Christian holidays.

As Christians, they have largely been left without the assistance of the region's Muslim powers, interested mainly in the protection of their coreligionists. Likewise, they are forgotten by American evangelical Christians whose pro-Israel, pro-bring-on-Armageddon views leave little room for the plight of a persecuted group of Christians.

This has left the community with little hope and thousands, particularly young people, have left the region in recent years, raising concern that this ancient community may not survive.

This desperation, by the way, has not gone unnoticed by Russia. In response, the Russian Orthodox Church has courted the Patriarchate of Jerusalem in its ongoing struggle with the Ecumenical Patriarchate of Constantinople for control of the Orthodox world, offering vague (and probably unreliable) offers of protection. And they have had some success.

The Patriarchate of Jerusalem is one of the few Orthodox jurisdictions that has not moved to name Russia as the aggressor in the conflict or offer outright condemnation of the invasion. It is a difficult position that puts them at odds not only with a large swathe of the Orthodox Christian world, but with many Palestinians who had hoped (perhaps without reason) that they could leverage the global response to the Russian invasion of Ukraine to draw attention to the perceived abuse of Palestinians by the Israeli government and perhaps obtain similar global condemnation for those abuses, including sanctions.

Few would envy the position of the Holy Land's native Christian population faced with two terrible choices: side with the world community against Russia and remain invisible, or side with Russia, the only entity that has even offered hope for support (however unlikely). It is clear they are not a priority for other Palestinians or for Christians outside of Israel – Orthodox or otherwise.

In the Gordian knot that is the Israeli–Palestinian conflict, they are the forgotten thread. But they are an excellent, living example, of the fraught modern history of Orthodox Christian communities, a history that involves real oppression and marginalization.

This is important because this real history feeds hysterical political narratives like those we are seeing come from the mouths of Vladimir Putin and Patriarch Kirill. Claims that dark forces (including 'the West', LGBT people, NATO and Jews) are plotting to destroy Orthodox Christianity appear to be legitimated when these kinds of things happen within the walls of Jerusalem. The best way to combat this conspiracy rhetoric is to address the real concerns of Eastern Christians as they emerge. And that means having to pay attention to hotels in Jerusalem's Old City.

May 5, 2022

Is this tiny, divided Orthodox nation the next front in Russia's religious war?

I am writing from Iași, Romania, which was the capital of the Principality of Moldova between 1564 and 1859 and the capital of Romania between 1916 and 1918, as well as the seat of the Romanian Orthodox Metropolitan of Moldavia and Bukovina. It is also about 225 miles from the city of Tiraspol, which is sort of in Moldova (more on that later), where, last week, explosions shook the Ministry of State Security and awakened fears that a new front might be opening in Russia's campaign of aggression in its former sphere of influence.

There is legitimate concern that if Moldova is the next country to come under Russian attack, Romania (a NATO member) will, as a result of its close historical, cultural and political ties to Moldova, be drawn into the conflict. This could, in turn, grant Vladimir Putin his longed-for showdown with NATO and likely grant the rest of us a Third World War.

It is a rather unnerving thought as I sit here, looking out across the balcony of my rented flat at a grey sky and the glittering crosses that adorn the top of Iași's imposing Metropolitan Cathedral.

Moldova was always among the three most likely places Putin would strike next, along with Estonia and the Republic of Georgia. All have breakaway regions with large Russian-speaking populations and historical ties to both the Russian Empire and the Soviet Union; and all are the site of complex jurisdictional conflicts between the Moscow-based Russian Orthodox Church (ROC) and local independent Orthodox bishops, usually acting with the support of the Patriarchate of Constantinople, a kind of 'Rebel Alliance' to the ROC's 'Empire' (to borrow an unapologetically heavy-handed Star Wars metaphor).

The conflicts among Orthodox bishops in Moldova have received much less attention than similar conflicts in Ukraine, even from the Orthodox media, but the situation bears some striking similarities. First, it is important to remember that the territory that currently makes up Moldova has at various points been under Ottoman, Polish, Romanian and Russian control.

In 1401, the autonomous Metropolis of Moldova was established by the Ecumenical Patriarch of Constantinople, with its seat in Iaşi. What is today eastern Romania and all of Moldova were under the Metropolis of Moldova until Bessarabia was annexed by the Russian Empire in 1812. (Bessarabia, located in eastern Moldova, is the region that is currently under dispute.) When this occurred, the Russian Orthodox Church took control of the churches and monasteries in the region and the local clergy came under the control of Moscow.

In 1918, in the wake of the Russian Revolution, the Russian Patriarch Tikhon gave the Moldovan Church the choice of uniting with either the Romanian Orthodox Church or the Russian Orthodox Church. The former was chosen.

However, when Moldova became independent in 1991 following the collapse of the Soviet Union, having seemingly forgotten the events of 1918, the Patriarchate of Moscow established the Metropolis of Chişinău and All Moldova, an autonomous but not independent jurisdiction. In the confounding structure of the Orthodox Church, this means that the metropolis has its own council of bishops (called a synod) but the ROC has the final say over who the chief bishop is.

Just a year later, however, a group of clergymen, unhappy with the new metropolis – and, seemingly, its metropolitan – asked to join the Romanian Orthodox Church. This request was granted by the Patriarch of Romania, who established the Metropolis of Bessarabia. The Moldovan government initially resisted recognizing the new metropolis, but was forced to by the European Court of Human Rights following a lengthy legal battle.

Today, the Russian-aligned Metropolis of Chişinău and All Moldova remains the majority Church by a large margin, but there is little doubt that Metropolitan Petru of Bessarabia, the head of the Romanian-connected Church, has used the Russian invasion of Ukraine to strengthen his position in a country rightly nervous about Russian hostility.

In his recent Easter message, Metropolitan Petru declared that war is caused by 'injustice, violence, disregard, lack of freedom and dignity, oppression and the desire to become more powerful than others'. This statement places him in direct opposition to Patriarch Kirill, not least by rejecting Kirill's claim that the Russian fight was a 'metaphysical battle' necessitated by evil forces, and by implicitly insisting that the war is the result of Russian oppression and power lust.

It is a message that, in addition to being true, could very well have deep resonance with a Russia-leery Moldovan population. Meanwhile, Petru's rival, Metropolitan Vladimir, the head of the Metropolis of Chişinău and All Moldova, made only oblique references to the current crisis in his Easter message, walking the thin line that so many Russia-aligned clerics outside of Russia walk these days.

I wrote on the eve of the Russian invasion of Ukraine that any war between Russia and Ukraine would be a religious war. The same is true for Moldova (and would, for that matter, also be true for Estonia and Georgia), because the current recurrence of

Russian aggression is intimately linked to the intra-Orthodox conflict over liberalism and modernity that extends across the Orthodox world, that mirrors so much of what we saw within Islam, at the turn of the century.

The places in which the Orthodox Church is embroiled in ecclesiastical conflict are the hotspots in this battle including, one could argue, the USA. In turn, these are also regions of great importance in the global Culture Wars, pointing to the fact that the Christian East in general, and Orthodox Christianity in particular, have a unique and significant role to play in this emerging global struggle. A cultural zone long in the shadow of its Western brother to the Christian East, so long obsessed with its medieval past, has now been thrust, willingly or not, into the centre of a very modern battle.

Sadly Ukraine is not the end of this battle. It is very likely just the beginning. And if the next chapter is Moldova there will be another set of Orthodox bishops' names and allegiances to memorize and medieval and early modern history to take down from the shelves.

May 22, 2022

Independence for the Ohrid archdioceses is more about Russia than Macedonia

There is one more independent Orthodox Church in the world today after the Patriarch of Belgrade recognized the independence of what he has chosen to call the 'Orthodox Church of (Northern) Macedonia'. The Serbian cleric's announcement comes weeks after a similar announcement by the Ecumenical Patriarch of Constantinople, marking a rare moment of agreement in an Orthodox world increasingly divided between those loyal to the Patriarchate of Moscow and those loyal to the Patriarchate of Constantinople.

The Church that both the Greek and Serbian Patriarchs agree is now independent dates back to the eleventh century and the Byzantine conquest of the Bulgarian Empire. Established as an independent archbishopric, that independence was revoked in 1767 by the Patriarch of Constantinople, part of the Ottoman-captive Patriarch's attempt to survive by expanding his sphere of influence (an effort that, for better or for worse, proved successful). The jurisdiction was revived at the end of the Second World War and renamed the Macedonian Orthodox Church, beginning a decades-long, often frustrated campaign for independence and recognition that culminated this week.

That this nearly 80-year-old quest would end now, just months after Russia's invasion of Ukraine is far from a coincidence. As the war in Ukraine demonstrates in stark and horrific terms, the Orthodox Christian world finds itself in the midst of an existential internal conflict, one in which the weight of history and a failure to reconcile with modernity have created ecclesiastical chaos that not infrequently leads to geopolitical conflict. For example, it is worth noting that, while the Serbian Orthodox Church was happy to call the Macedonian Church the Orthodox Church of (Northern) Macedonia', the Greek Ecumenical Patriarch has chosen to use the medieval name, 'Archdiocese of Ohrid'. The latter's choice is no doubt the result of the conflict between Greece and Northern Macedonia over the Macedonians' use of the name *Macedonia*, a name it shares with an ancient Greek province that was home to Alexander the Great.

For its part, the Russian Church has kept an interested distance from the situation in Northern Macedonia. The Russians have condemned the Ecumenical Patriarch's decision to intervene, calling it 'an irregular and politically motivated intrusion'. Not that anyone in Moscow cares about the fate of this small Church in an even less significant former Yugoslavian republic. When the Russian clerics decry 'an irregular and politically motivated intrusion' they are really thinking about Ukraine and the Ecumenical Patriarch's meddling there in 2018 when he established the Orthodox Church of Ukraine, an independent Church that exists in Ukraine today alongside the much larger Moscow-linked Ukrainian Orthodox Church, the alleged persecution of which forms one of Russia's key stated motives for invasion. Against this backdrop what Russia chooses to do in Northern Macedonia might send some signals about its intentions in Ukraine.[2]

For now, the Orthodox Church of Macedonia will have its independence. Whether that independence will remain is another question entirely.

---

2 The Russian Orthodox Church acknowledged the independence of the Orthodox Church of Macedonia in August 2022. In doing so, ROC acknowledged the Serbian Orthodox Church as the Mother Church of Macedonia, intentionally ignoring the role of the Ecumenical Patriarch.

June 14, 2022

Is the worldwide Russian Orthodox Church looking to Westernize?

A major shake-up at the highest levels in the Russian Orthodox Church is offering new insight into the Moscow-based Church's internal struggles and strategic position towards the West – and oddly no one in the West seems to care.

Metropolitan Hilarion (Alfeyev) has been dismissed from his duties as Metropolitan of Volokolamsk and as the head of the Russian Orthodox Church's powerful Department of External Relations. Previously considered to be the most likely successor to Patriarch Kirill, Metropolitan Hilarion had attempted in recent weeks to distance himself from Patriarch Kirill's most inflammatory rhetoric with regard to the war in Ukraine.

While no official reason has been given for the move, for his part Metropolitan Hilarion has speculated that it was because he could no longer 'fit' given the current geopolitical situation, an allusion to his less than enthusiastic public support for the Russian invasion of Ukraine. But even his explanation might be considered part of the influential bishop's plan to secure himself a future should Putin and Patriarch Kirill ultimately fall. And he is still quite well positioned for such an eventuality.

Metropolitan Hilarion will now become the primate of the Russian Orthodox Dioceses of Budapest and Hungary, an interesting choice indeed considering Russia's increasing friendliness with Hungary's far-right leader, Viktor Orban.

While on the one hand it is easy to understand the move as an attempt on the part of the Russian Patriarch to exile a powerful and ambitious rival (this is clearly a demotion, make no mistake about it), it is, on the other hand, also noteworthy that he is being cast out into the court of an important ally. Orban is, after all, arguably Russia's main ally within the European Union, single handedly holding back an EU-ban on the importation of Russian oil.

Orban's Hungary and the Russian Orthodox Church also have an important and powerful ally: American right-wing evangelicals, creating a Christian right axis that unites Eastern Europe, Western Europe and North America: Orthodox, Catholic and Protestant. Moreover, let us not forget, Metropolitan Hilarion will now be a legal resident of the European Union. Moving him to Budapest does not remove him from the centre of power, it places him right in the middle of it – whether his Patriarch can see that now or not.

Importantly, Metropolitan Hilarion's replacement at the Department of External Relations is a man with his feet firmly outside of Russia as well. Metropolitan Anthony (Sevryuk) was until now the head of the Patriarchal Exarchate of Western Europe. Created in 2018, in direct response to the ecclesiastical battle between Moscow and Constantinople in Ukraine, the jurisdiction was created just as the Russian Orthodox Church set up rivals to the Patriarchate of Constantinople in Spain and Portugal and in Southeast Asia.

At the time, Metropolitan Hilarion explicitly stated that, with the creation of the new Church bodies, the Russian Orthodox Church would 'act as if they [i.e. the Patriarchate of Constantinople] do not exist at all', a sort of declaration of war against the Ecumenical Patriarch and a clear indication of the Russian Orthodox Church's intention to lead the Orthodox world, both inside and outside the diaspora.

With his accession to the leadership of the Department of External Relations, which carries with it a place in the Holy Synod of the Russian Orthodox Church (the Church's ruling council of bishops), the 37-year-old Metropolitan Anthony now occupies the place largely considered to be the holding pen for the next Russian Patriarch. The vast majority of his life has been lived in post-Soviet Russia and he has spent the majority of his career in Western Europe, including in Rome and Paris. One would hope that this would make him a more open, progressive (in relative terms) and cosmopolitan cleric than Patriarch Kirill or Metropolitan Hilarion, both of whom were shaped by the gruelling realities and harsh isolation of the Soviet period.

But the very fact of his elevation suggests that this hope might be false. Patriarch Kirill is a man under siege, and the Church he leads is one that is arguably increasingly isolated, finding itself among hostiles in what was once friendly territory. It seems highly unlikely that he would bring into his inner circle a man about whose loyalty he was not 100 per cent certain. Moreover, there is, without a doubt, a diaspora effect – the reality that those living outside the Mother Country are often prone to an increased kind of conservatism, resulting from the experience of living as a 'stranger in a strange land'.

What very well might be happening is that, in Metropolitan Anthony, Patriarch Kirill and the Russian Orthodox Church have found a true believer who also has an intimate familiarity with 'enemy territory'. In short, Metropolitan Anthony's elevation is proof that the Russian Orthodox Church remains very interested in the West, and probably not in a 'getting to know you' kind of way.

Certainly, it is difficult, in light of everything else going on, to want to pay much attention to the Byzantine machinations of the Russian Orthodox Church and the wider Orthodox world. The average Westerner's lack of familiarity with the structures and roles involved in this medieval game of thrones undoubtedly plays a role in this; however, as has been said before, the Russian Orthodox Church is a tool of the Russian state, an instrument of Russian soft power. Understanding the inner workings of the Russian Church is crucial to understanding what exactly the Russian Federation is up to.

Today, one of the Russian Church's most powerful men has been sent into exile and into the heart of the Christian far-right's global alliance, and one of its young bishops has been called back from the decadent West to be the crown prince. You might want to pay attention to that.

November 17, 2022

As tensions mount in the Balkans, the West could hand Putin a valuable weapon

Large crowds of ethnic Serbs recently gathered to demonstrate against a plan by the Kosovar government to gradually ban Serbia-issued number plates, while over 300 ethnic Serbs have resigned from the police force in the majority-Serb province of North Mitrovica, as part of a larger withdrawal of Serbians from the province's public institutions.

The dispute is the latest in a series of escalations in the region which, though eerily reminiscent of the 1990s, have been widely overshadowed in the Western media by the war in Ukraine. Yet this is an oversight that could have dire consequences in the near future, as a second war, not entirely unrelated to the current war, threatens to break out in the heart of Europe.

The lack of sufficient attention to developments in the Balkans demonstrates not only our propensity to ignore brewing trouble but also the West's enduring failure to view the Orthodox Christian cultural zone as a continuous cultural and political region – not unlike the 'Islamic World' – best understood as a whole, even while appreciating the diversity that exists within it. This way of viewing the region would inevitably prevent the armchair analysis of the Kosovo situation, such as it exists, that merely reduces to a glib analysis of Serbians as 'pro-Putin' as a means of explaining all the trouble brewing in the Balkans.

In fact, polling suggests that only a little more than one in five Serbs describe themselves as supporters of Putin's Russia in foreign policy, while half support continuing the Yugoslav-era policy of non-alignment. It is not support for Russia or Putin which motivates the anti-Western attitude among young Serbs today, but rather a feeling that Serbia was wronged by the West during the Yugoslav and Kosovo Wars in the 1990s – a wrong that many see as emerging from the West's wilful misunderstanding of the region's history.

So, here is a one-paragraph summary of a history that you probably did not hear in school, but now need to learn ASAP:

During the Middle Ages, Kosovo was the political, cultural and religious centre of the Serbian Empire and the Serbs were the dominant ethnic group in the multi-ethnic Balkans. However, between 1299 and 1453, the Ottoman Empire conquered much of the Orthodox Christian world – including the Serbian Empire – and the Albanians converted to Islam, greatly elevating their status in an empire in which Muslims were most certainly at the top of the pecking order.

This is the origin of much of the anti-Albanian sentiment, not only in Serbia, but throughout the Balkans. It is also at the heart of the Serbian claim to Kosovo, which is unquestionably the birthplace of Serbian Orthodoxy and the heartland of medieval Serbia. In addition, the sense that it is ultimately the Serbs who have been, in the broad view of history, displaced and targeted for genocide is the principal reason that, even decades later, Serbian society writ large has done little to confront or condemn the Serbian-perpetuated genocide against Albanian Kosovars in the late 1990s.

The fact is a significant number of Serbs, and even a large number of others from traditionally Orthodox backgrounds, continue to nurse a great deal of anger about Western intervention in the Kosovo War, which they see as a failure by the West to comprehend the historical role reversal that had taken place, including the persecution of Orthodox Christians by Albanians and other majority-Muslim ethnic groups during the Ottoman period. From their perspective, it is as though the West jumped into the movie just as the underdog had risen up to fight the big baddy – and then taken the latter's side.

And while it clearly does not justify genocide, their sense of injustice is not entirely without basis. The general Western ignorance concerning the collective history of the Orthodox Christian culture zone is a problem, particularly with respect to the formative Ottoman period. This is the case, in no small part, because, for most Westerners, 'the Ottoman Empire' seems like some medieval thing that happened a long time ago. Consequently, complaining about events during the Ottoman period feels to them like making a big deal about the Anglo-Saxon invasion of England (which people do, by the way, if indirectly; think of the Scottish and Welsh independence movements).

The fact is, however, that the Ottoman Empire survived into the early twentieth century, only collapsing after the First World War. Most of the Balkans became independent in the nineteenth century. The nation state of Greece is only 201 years old and did not include most of the historically Greek regions at its formation. I am not yet 40 years old and I have great-grandparents (one of whom I knew as a young child) who were born and spent their lives into early adulthood in the Ottoman Empire.

In fact, I can easily think of more than a dozen people I have known who were born under Ottoman rule, some of whom died only recently. The Ottoman occupation of majority Orthodox Christian populations and historical Orthodox Christian territory is, in most cases, as recent or more recent than American chattel slavery. And only the ignorant or ideologically motivated (i.e. racist) would argue that American chattel slavery has no effect today.

The failure of the West to understand this recent history and to take it into account in the analysis of current events is the very opening that Russia is looking for when it seeks to wield influence in places like Serbia, where people are not necessarily thrilled at the prospect of Russian domination, but where there is deep mistrust of a West that seems completely unaware of the historical memories at play.

Russia has been more than happy to fill the gap. Russian propaganda network RT recently launched a local website and broadcaster in Serbia. Offering a mildly bizarre but strangely predictable explanation for the expansion, RT chief editor Margarita Simonyan tweeted: 'We have launched RT in the Balkans. Because Kosovo is Serbia.'

This opportunism can also be seen in a recent meme, largely in Russian, repurposing a nearly 40-year-old slogan, which declares in various ways: 'Everything is Russia, except Kosovo. Kosovo is Serbia.' It is a not-so-subtle message to the Serbian people: 'Russia gets it. And a world with Russia in charge will see Kosovo returned to you.' What does the West have to offer?

This ignorance also offers Russia and other reactionaries a valuable weapon in their efforts to win new converts, allowing them to argue that there is a 'hidden history' of Christian persecution and suffering that is being kept from them. And there is evidence that these efforts are already afoot. Early in 2021 the National Catholic Register, a conservative publication, ran a piece entitled 'The Silent Persecution of Christians in Kosovo', which, while undeniably biased, was not entirely untrue. Likewise, in September, in a piece for *The American Conservative* about the war in Ukraine, Doug Bandow called on readers to 'witness NATO's aggressive war against Serbia over Kosovo'.

On 4 November 2022, International Family News, a right-wing website run by National Organization for Marriage president Brian Brown, ran a piece entitled 'Spread the word, resist the ideological colonization' praising Serbia's violent rejection of EuroPride and framing the Serbian people as heroically standing against the West and its dangerous, sinful world-view. A new Russia, if you will, but made sympathetic to Western eyes. This is all possible in no small part because Westerners have missed much of the nuance in the history of the conflict in Kosovo. Any way you look at it, this is a dangerous lacuna in our view of history.

If you find it hard to have sympathy for those you associate with genocidaires (i.e. the Serbs) expressing anger towards the former victims of that genocide (the Albanians) for not wanting to look at Serbian number plates any more, you need to be aware that there is a longer history here. If you only know part of the story, the story seems much more one sided. This failure to see the more complex history plays right into the hands of the Putin regime. Simply ignoring what is happening in the Balkans, as the Western media seems to be doing, is a recipe for another war.

December 24, 2022

In Cyprus's search for a new archbishop Russia did not get its way

Cyprus has a new archbishop and an attempt by Russia to place a puppet on the episcopal throne of Cyprus has been thwarted.

Archbishop Chrysostomos II, who had been the head of the independent Church of Cyprus since 2006, had drawn considerable attention for his often reactionary views and tacit (and sometimes not so tacit) support for far-right causes. He routinely drew criticism for his support of the far-right ultranationalist ELAM (National People's Front), a political party that has been associated with a number of violent incidents. He answered charges of racism in part by declaring that he 'would even vote for a Black man' who shared his views.

Following the Turkish government's decision to reconvert the Hagia Sophia into a mosque the Archbishop, seemingly oblivious to the ethnic tensions that grip the island in his care, avoided the conciliatory tone taken by many, including Orthodox clerics, declaring:

> The Turks have remained uncivilized, they are rude, and they will remain [this way]. Turkey has learned to destroy, it has learned to appropriate the cultures of others and sometimes, when it does not benefit it, it destroys them and falsely presents [other] cultures as its own.

The archbishop was also an outspoken critic of LGBT rights, calling the Cypriot government's introduction of legislation to recognize same-sex partnerships a sign of 'weakening moral integrity'. In 2016, he announced that the Church of Cyprus had established its own school system, seemingly for the sole purpose of teaching that homosexuality was unnatural.

This is all to say that Archbishop Chrysostomos II seemed like the exact kind of cleric whom Russia could rely upon as part of its network of far-right advocates. Except that was not the case. Chrysostomos II was not that very contemporary creature, 'a global traditionalist'. While it has become normal to assume religious and political figures will cluster together around a shared social agenda, with issues of race and sexuality at the top of the list of important shared values, the head of the Cypriot Church broke this model. He was not a 'global traditionalist', but instead what one might call a 'Byzantine Nationalist'. Seemingly oblivious to the battle lines of contemporary wars, cultural and literal, Chrysostomos II was most concerned with the memory of an imagined Byzantine past, a world whose social, moral and cultural centre was populated by *Greek* Orthodox Christians. Thus, it is natural that he was a reliable ally of the Ecumenical Patriarchate of Constantinople, supporting the establishment of an independent Church in Ukraine and opposing Russian incursion into 'Greek' territory whenever possible. This was true even though he had deep and abiding disagreements with the Istanbul-based Patriarch, who is widely regarded as pro-Western and 'modernizing'.

His death then opened an opportunity for Russia to place an ally at the head of an important, ethnically Greek Church. And it was a unique opportunity. Thanks to reforms introduced by Chrysostomos II (who was for better or worse a populist in his own way), the process of selecting an Archbishop of Cyprus is oddly democratic for the Orthodox world. Instead of a clandestine, Byzantine process solely in the hands of bishops, in Cyprus an election is held to select the three candidates whom the bishops can consider for the post. In other words, the Orthodox Christian faithful of Cyprus get to construct the short list. In theory, Orthodox Christians of any nationality who have been resident on Cyprus are eligible to vote, and many of those non-Cypriot Orthodox Christians are Russians. In 2018, the *Guardian* suggested there might be around 50,000 Russians living in Cyprus, a not insignificant number on a small island in an election which was going to have a poor turn out from the start. (In the end only 30 per cent of eligible voters bothered to show up at the polls.)

It was clear that something had to be done to keep out Russian interference. Thus it was announced at the end of November that the voter rolls for the archiepiscopal election would be obtained from the state and that there was simply not enough time to add foreign believers to the list. It was a transparent dodge. And a necessary one. Among the leading candidates was Metropolitan Athanasios of Limassol. As the presiding hierarch of a city known for its strong Russian presence, Metropolitan Athanasios is widely known for his pro-Russian sentiments. He had a Russian-style church built in his diocese with money from Russian oligarchs and won criticism from Chrysostomos II for presiding at a liturgy in honour of Tsar Nicholas II, the last Russian monarch. In a telling twist, even with Russians and other foreigners excluded from the polls, it was Metropolitan Athanasios who won a plurality of the votes in the popular election.

In the end, however, George (Papachrysostomou), formerly the Metropolitan of Paphos, who had come in a distant second in the popular election, was selected by the Holy Synod to become Archbishop of Cyprus. Now Archbishop George III is an outspoken opponent of Russia and the Moscow-based Church's efforts to exert their influence around the world.

It is a rather uncomfortable end to the story that points to the deep divisions that run across the Orthodox world, lines that do not divide across ethnic, national or even political frontiers. Over 30 per cent of the Orthodox faithful of EU- and NATO-member Cyprus voted for a staunchly pro-Russian bishop to be their leader. It was only because the other bishops on the island stepped in and essentially overrode the will of the people, selecting a candidate that got nearly half the number of votes, that the Church of Cyprus is now not in the hands of a pro-Russian archbishop. That should be a sobering message to the world. A message that we simply cannot afford to ignore.

January 5, 2023

The Korean Peninsula: the next front in Russia's quest to be an Orthodox influencer

The omnipresence of ethnic divides is a reality for the Orthodox diaspora. In most places outside of its traditional homelands, Orthodox Christianity has arrived as the faith of immigrants, not missionaries. Orthodox churches were founded in a rather haphazard manner as a result, as individual communities sent home for priests on an as-needed basis. These priests were each under the authority of their local bishops, and when the time to have local bishops arrived, different ethnic communities invariably set up their own dioceses and archdioceses. As a result, in most of the world, Orthodox churches exist with what is delicately termed 'overlapping jurisdictions'. That is to say, Orthodox churches exist in the same geographic territory under the authority of different bishops.

The Korean peninsula seemed to be the one place where these patterns were broken. However, now it too has fallen victim to the growing war between Constantinople and Moscow and Russian efforts to deploy the Russian Orthodox Church as an extension of its global power.

Perhaps this should come as no surprise, given that Orthodoxy arrived in Korea for that very reason. In 1900, the Russian Empire sent its first Orthodox missionaries to Korea, led by Archimandrite Chrysanthos Shehtkofsky. The missionaries were seeking to win souls not just for Christ, but for

Russia. Within 17 years the mission employed 12 Russians and 17 Koreans, who served a few hundred converts across the country. The first ethnic Korean priest was ordained in 1912. It was, as Orthodoxy's missionary efforts have historically been, quite successful.

And then came the October Revolution of 1917.

Overnight the mission was cut off from its financial and logistical support. Within a year just one Russian priest and two Korean school teachers remained at the mission. Yet somehow, the small Orthodox community survived. When the last Russian priest left the country in 1947, an ethnic Korean, Alexei Kim Ui-han, was ordained to the priesthood. The only remaining Orthodox priest in the country. The outbreak of the Korean War in 1950 only made matters worse, as whatever remained of organized religious life was thrown into complete chaos by the war; yet, it may also have been the Korean War that saved Korea's Orthodox Community.

In 1953, Archimandrite Andreas Halkiopoulos, a Greek army chaplain stationed in Korea, learned about the abandoned Korean Orthodox community. Father Andreas set to work, leveraging support from the Church of Greece and the Greek diaspora to re-establish a parish in Seoul. The following year an ethnic Korean, Boris Moon Yee-chun, was ordained to the priesthood. The war prevented the usual pattern of missionary work with Orthodoxy, a pattern where priests are for decades drawn from traditionally Orthodox ethnic groups and the 'mother country', frequently excluding the native born from leadership in the Church.

At Christmas 1955, the Seoul parish voted unanimously to join the Ecumenical Patriarchate. Since then, there has been one jurisdiction in Korea and a vibrant, multi-ethnic Korean Orthodox community has grown to include seven parishes, two monasteries, a publishing house, two bookshops and a kindergarten, all staffed and attended by a mix of ethnic Koreans and Russian, Greek, Romanian and Serbian expats. A model for what Orthodoxy in the diaspora might look like.

That was until 2018.

As in many parts of the world, the Russian Orthodox Church reacted to the Ecumenical Patriarchate's decision to establish an independent Church in Ukraine by setting up their own alternative churches in territory long considered Constantinople's domain. At Christmas 2018, Moscow established the Diocese of South and North Korea, a name that hints at the Russian Orthodox Churches other, arguably much more nefarious, post-Soviet activities in the Korean Peninsula.

The Ecumenical Patriarchate, respecting the common belief of Koreans, has chosen to call the Korean jurisdiction the 'Metropolis of Korea', a nod to the belief that Korea is one nation only temporarily divided. Moreover, the Ecumenical Patriarchate, at the behest of the Korean faithful and in keeping with its own self-image as a proponent of religious freedom around the world, has refused to co-operate with the North Korean government in establishing a puppet Church in the North. Thus, when the North Korean regime started looking for an Orthodox bishop to lend legitimacy to its plans for an Orthodox Church in the country, it looked to Moscow.

Religious organizations are tightly controlled in the official atheist totalitarian state of North Korea. While it is nearly impossible to know what exactly has happened to religious communities there over the past 70 years, many experts have suggested that, as opposed to complete repression, the Kim regime's strategic allowance of some loyal religious expression has prevented any large-scale dissent from arising around the religious question. Kim Il Sung in particular seemed eager to encourage a certain kind of tightly controlled religious expression.

It was Kim's successor who decided to build an Orthodox church in Pyongyang following a 2002 trip to Russia. As an indication of the religious situation in North Korea, when a Russian diplomat asked whether there were any Orthodox believers in the country, the North Korean dictator ominously replied that they 'could be found'.

By the next year, four students had been sent from North Korea to the Moscow Ecclesiastical Seminary to train as priests. All the seminarians were former employees of the North Korean Intelligence Service. In 2006, the Church of the Life-Giving Trinity, a parish of the Patriarchate of Moscow, opened in Pyongyang. It is reported that very few locals and only a handful of Russian diplomats stationed in the country ever attend the services.

The twenty-first-century Russian foray into North Korea highlights the transparent cynicism of the Moscow Patriarchate's efforts on behalf of the Russian state. Certainly, no one seriously believes that the Church of the Life-Giving Trinity represents a genuine missionary effort. Much worse, by engaging with the Kim regime, the Moscow Patriarchate is lending its legitimacy (such as it is at this point) to the appearance of tolerance that makes actual religious persecution in North Korea possible. At the same time, in the South, the Moscow Patriarchate seems committed to allowing its jurisdictional war with Constantinople to completely upend one of the most successful Orthodox missions in history. There simply is no ecclesiastical or theological justification for these actions. These are clearly actions motivated by the demands of cut-throat geopolitics and nothing else, and they give the lie to any air of respectability or independence the Moscow-based Church may try to project.

Should anyone be in doubt about the real objectives of the Russian Orthodox Church outside of Russia they need only look to Korea.

January 8, 2023

Russia's man in Cyprus

While speaking at a primary school (yes, a primary school) in July 2019, Bishop Neophytos (Masouras) of Morpou, a prominent bishop within the Orthodox Church of Cyprus, posited that a boy will be gay if the child's mother has anal sex during her pregnancy; although, only if she liked it. He attributes his theory to St Porphyrios of Kafsokalivia, a twentieth-century monk who spent the first and last years of his life on Mount Athos, a self-governing monastic community in the Aegean where women are forbidden. Numerous collections of Porphyria's teachings have been compiled and published since his death in 1991. Despite this, I was unable to track down the particular theory referenced by Bishop Neophytos. Not that I am doubting the bishop; however, considering other things he has said, it seems unfair to immediately blame poor St Porphyrios.

Curious speculations about the epigenetic effects of anal sex are not the only alarming views to be expressed by the high-profile cleric from the village of Ano Zodhia. Reactionary even in the context of the deeply conservative Church of Cyprus, Bishop Neophytos has in recent years drawn increasingly closer to the Russian Church, providing them with a useful stooge in their ongoing struggle against the Greek Patriarchate of Constantinople.

For example, he has been an opponent of the establishment of the Orthodox Church of Ukraine by the Ecumenical Patriarch, a rare position within the Hellenic world, where the universal authority of the Patriarchate of Constantinople is commonly recognized. For Bishop Neophytos, however, Patriarch Bartholomew's intervention in Ukraine was not a sign of the Istanbul-based hierarch reclaiming his rightful place in global Christendom, it was evidence that the Patriarch of Constantinople was in the thrall of nefarious influences: the bishop has made his position clear in terms that clearly mark him out as a reactionary Orthodox Christian bishop of a certain variety:

> Personally, I think this is already a difficult task (*note: recognizing the independence of the Orthodox Church of Ukraine*), since the Ecumenical Patriarchate, solely for geostrategic, geopolitical reasons, within the framework of the New World Order, has recognized as the new primate a person who comes from a schismatic group of non-ordained people (meaning without the Holy Spirit).

Furthermore, unlike most other Greek clerics, be they connected to the Church of Greece, the Church of Cyprus or the Patriarchate of Constantinople, Bishop Neophytos has not condemned the Russian invasion of Ukraine, saying it was a 'necessary operation' needed to purge away the 'devil children' created by modern liberalism. In pinning blame for the war on the necessity of the Orthodox faithful to eradicate the evils wrought by liberalism and pluralism, the Cypriot bishop was in some ways foreshadowing the rhetoric that would quickly be adopted by Patriarch Kirill, the head of the Russian Orthodox Church.

And now, after failing to even make the short list for the job, the bishop has refused to attend the enthronement of the new Archbishop of Cyprus, saying that he would instead be in his 'humble cell' praying for the 'persecuted churches in Ukraine' – a reference to recent crackdowns in Ukraine against the Moscow-backed Ukrainian Orthodox Church, suspected by many to be operating as a cover for Russian espionage.

It is a dramatic and public act of defiance that demonstrates the ways in which the fissures in the Orthodox world, as they grow more intense, are no longer respecting old lines. Like the rest of the world, the Orthodox Church seems increasingly to be abandoning the old lines of loyalty in favour of clustering together with those with whom one might share little else than a position in the global Culture Wars. It is a disorienting reality, one that plays directly into the hands of some of the world's worst and most violent actors.

Part 4

THE WAR WILL END BUT THE CAUSES AND CONSEQUENCES WILL REMAIN, SO WHAT CAN BE DONE?

March 4, 2022

A Church (further) divided: Putin's Patriarch faces a rebellion from within the Russian Orthodox Church

While the world waits for Russian oligarchs to tire of their yachts being seized and for them to turn against Vladimir Putin, it appears that Putin's counterpart and accomplice in the Russian Orthodox Church, Patriarch Kirill of Moscow and All Rus, is already facing a rebellion from within, pointing once again to the deep divides that animate the Orthodox Christian world – both inside and outside of Russia – and play a significant role in the continuing conflict in Ukraine.

Despite what some in the Western press have been willing to believe, Patriarch Kirill has not been an advocate for peace. In fact, he has at times seemingly gone out of his way to provoke the situation, conjuring the memory of old hatreds and false histories. This has stood in sharp contrast to many, if not most, of the responses from Orthodox Christian leaders around the world. That said, the Church of Bulgaria, the Church of Serbia and the Church of Jerusalem all seem uncertain who the aggressor is, while Metropolitan Hilarion, the head of the independent, US-based, Russian Orthodox Church Outside of Russia (ROCOR), decided to use his statement to make comments that seemingly undermine Ukrainian sovereignty. Still, many Orthodox Christian leaders, including the Ecumenical

Patriarch of Constantinople, have been explicit in their criticism of Putin and his invasion.

While these differences speak to the conflict between Orthodox jurisdictions around the world, Kirill is now experiencing public dissent from his pro-Putin position from within his own fiefdom.

Hundreds of Russian clerics have signed a letter calling for an end to the war in Ukraine, a rare show of opposition from the Russian Orthodox Church inside Russia. Moreover, and perhaps even more threatening to Kirill's and Putin's long-term ambitions, a number of outposts of the Moscow Patriarchate abroad (including those in Ukraine) have shown clear signs of wanting to make a formal break.

Most explicitly, priests in the Ukrainian Archdiocese of Lviv, which remains part of the Moscow Patriarchate, have sent an open letter to their local bishop asking that a council be called to contemplate their independence from Moscow. Other priests have ceased 'commemorating' Kirill – in other words, they have stopped acknowledging and praying for him during services. Typically, in the Orthodox world, the end of such prayers is a clear sign of schism, a break of one Church body with another.

But as Father Cyril Hovorun, a Ukrainian Orthodox priest and theologian, and one of the world's leading experts on political Orthodoxy, has noted, this may not be the case here. These are, after all, extraordinary circumstances. But after years of demanding that he, Patriarch Kirill, is the chief pastor of Ukraine, to the point of causing open rifts within the wider global Orthodox communion, these are damning failures.

However, schism or no schism, these instances of objection from within churches ostensibly under the authority of the Moscow Patriarchate suggest once again that this is not only a war between Russia and the West, but a war within Orthodoxy itself. While no one would expect people to easily pray for a faraway bishop seemingly indifferent to the fact that bombs are falling on them (as is precisely the case for Ukrainian Orthodox Christians under the Moscow Patriarchate at the moment), the fact that clerics within Russia seem to be publicly expressing dissatisfaction with Kirill's pastoral guidance is a bit more shocking.

While it might have been possible for years to see the current dispute within Orthodox Christianity as a revival of all the old cultural and national divides that have shaped so much in its history, what we are seeing here is truly an ideological contest that is cutting across those old divisions. This is a battle within Orthodoxy about what it means to be an Orthodox Christian in the twenty-first century. As of now, the winner remains unclear.

March 14, 2022

One prominent Russian Orthodox church rejects the pro-Putin Patriarch, raising tensions within the Orthodox world

The Russian Orthodox Church of St Nicholas in Amsterdam has a rather prominent place in the Orthodox Christian pacifist movement, insofar as such a movement exists. St Nicholas was, after all, the home parish of Jim Forest, an American writer and peace activist who converted to Orthodoxy. Forest first came to public attention as one of the 'Milwaukee Fourteen', a group of peace activists who burned selective service records to protest the Vietnam War. After his conversion, Forest would go on to help found the Orthodox Peace Fellowship, serving as its international secretary and the editor of its magazine *In Communion*. He was, in essence, the voice of the Orthodox Christian pacifist movement.

Jim Forest died earlier this year, but it would appear his legacy, including his willingness to run afoul of the authorities, continues at St Nicholas. Immediately following the Russian invasion of Ukraine, the clergy of St Nicholas, which was at this point, and for a long time before, a church under the Moscow Patriarchate, signed a petition asking Patriarch Kirill to call for an end to the violence.

Of course, he did not do that.

So on 4 March, St Nicholas's clergy sent a letter to Archbishop Elisey – essentially their middle manager – telling him that

Patriarch Kirill would no longer be commemorated at St Nicholas as a result of his failure to condemn the invasion. This means that during worship services they would no longer acknowledge him as their chief bishop or pray for him.

Two days later, on a Sunday, Archbishop Elisey arrived unannounced at St Nicholas (in a diplomatic car, according to church witnesses). He said his aim was to ensure that Patriarch Kirill would continue to be commemorated at St Nicholas. Then, after the service, he told the clergy that their dispute with Kirill was of great concern to the Russian Ministry of Foreign Affairs. The clergy of St Nicholas refused to relent.

It was at this point that the threats began. A service was interrupted by a man who broke a window; an online smear campaign was launched against the parish; and the church was vandalized with the pro-Putin, pro-war 'Z' symbol graffitied across the walls. Despite all this, the Archbishop inexplicably shared on social media that the situation at St Nicholas had been resolved.

On 12 March, after an emergency parish council meeting, St Nicholas announced that they had asked to leave the Moscow Patriarchate and join the Ecumenical Patriarchate of Constantinople, who was more than willing to accept them, suggesting that the Patriarchate of Constantinople may be abandoning attempts to appease Moscow by offering up Russian-tradition parishes in Western Europe. On 26 March, the whole parish council voted to leave Moscow. St Nicholas would go to Constantinople and one of the remaining progressive parishes in the Russian sphere would leave.

This very troubling situation should raise alarm bells far beyond Amsterdam. While Church and state remain officially separated in Russia, there is little doubt that, particularly over the past decade, the Russian Orthodox Church has increasingly become allied with the Russian state which has, in turn, deployed it as an instrument of Russian soft power around the world. Particularly under the circumstances, we would be remiss to forget that one of the reasons the Ukrainian government petitioned the Ecumenical Patriarch with such diligence for an independent Ukrainian Church was because of suspicions that Moscow Patriarchate churches were being used by the Russian state for espionage.

Furthermore, US Special Prosecutors, in their investigation of Russian state-sponsored hacking, found that senior non-Russian Orthodox clergy – most notably the Patriarch of Constantinople – had been targets. There were also concerns that the vast new Holy Trinity Cathedral, opened in Paris in 2016, would be used to spy on diplomats living nearby. This is all to say nothing of the fact that the Moscow Patriarchate's recent power grab in Africa, ostensibly motivated by the ecclesiastical crisis in Ukraine, has been suggested by some commentators to be a front for the FSB (essentially a post-soviet version of the KGB).

The most recent letter to the faithful published with the consent of the highest-ranking Moscow cleric in America makes it clear that they are well aware of concerns about espionage, though it is unclear whether they will do anything to address those, or whether they will simply double down. Abbot Nikodim writes, in part:

> And so what? Our fathers disregarded all the hardships of their time and were not afraid to remain faithful to the First Hierarch of Moscow, but today we are beginning to be ashamed of our position?

It seems clear that the Moscow-aligned bishops in America will not break with Kirill and, by extension, Putin. Certainly, that fact alone does not make them spies or otherwise agents of the Russian state, but it does reveal an unwillingness to acknowledge that there are serious problems here. The Russian Orthodox Church is not neutral in this war and this requires everyone thus associated, especially in an official capacity, to start making their own position clear.

Our concern, most assuredly, should not be with all Russian Orthodox clergy and certainly not with all the faithful. Many, both inside and outside Russia, have bravely spoken up against this war and the silence of their chief shepherd. But the events in Amsterdam cannot be ignored. Around the world, the Moscow Patriarchate frequently serves the interests of the Russian state. In light of recent events, there is no reason to believe that this will end and every reason to believe that it will become worse.

Additionally, the events in Amsterdam highlight the ways in which the ongoing conflict between the Patriarchate of Moscow and the Patriarchate of Constantinople is deeply intertwined with geopolitics and, now, the global Culture Wars. As much as this is a conflict between Russia and the West, it is also a conflict within Orthodoxy, in which not only the Russian Church but also the Russian state has a stake in keeping people and parishes on its side. As a consequence, it is a conflict that can no longer be ignored by those outside the Orthodox world. After all, you never know when a Russian archbishop might show up in a diplomatic car in a neighbourhood near you.

March 21, 2022

Failure to grasp the character and history of Eastern Christianity is compromising our understanding of Russia's invasion of Ukraine

Since the Russian invasion of Ukraine began, it is likely you've heard the term "Russian world" (*Russkiy mir*). It is easy to conflate this concept with nostalgia for the Soviet Union (it is just another term for Russia plus satellite states, right?), but the term – and the concept – predates the Soviet Union and Marx by centuries and it bears the mark of Orthodox Christian political philosophy and history. It has, subsequently, underscored much of Patriarch Kirill of Moscow's defence of the Russian invasion.

This is why it is significant that a declaration denouncing the concept of Russia World, with signatories from around the world – among them some of most important living Orthodox Christian theologians – appeared on the websites of two of the world's leading centres for Orthodox Christianity, Volos Academy for Theological Studies and the Centre for Orthodox Christian Studies at Fordham University.[3]

3 Disclosure: I have signed this declaration and I do believe the teaching of Russia World and other nationalists visions are heretical within the canonical and patristic tradition of the Orthodox Church. I also, however, recognize the prevalence of this kind of thinking within the history of Orthodox Christianity and in Orthodox Christian cultures. As I have tried to highlight before, there's an on-going debate in Orthodox Christianity. As a practising Orthodox Christian, I fall firmly on one side of that debate. As a historian, I acknowledge that the tradition is remarkably complex and provides evidence for multiple, frequently contradictory positions.

The Moscow Patriarchate has essentially responded through the personal website of Alexander Shipkov, one of its media liaisons. In the statement, Shipkov rejects the declaration published on 'a Greek portal' as a 'a purely political document that has nothing to do with genuine Christianity'.

It is merely the most recent flare-up of the conflict within the Orthodox Christian world over its relationship to liberalism and Western modernity more broadly – and it motivates so much of the rhetoric on, if not the actual invasion of, Ukraine. The skirmish over 'Russia World' in particular highlights the ways in which both sides of this conflict draw on legitimate elements of Orthodox Christian history and theology to support their position.

Moreover, it is clear that the two sides are speaking primarily to one another, and not to the Western world whose values and norms are ostensibly at the centre of this debate, as they call on events, thinkers and practices virtually unknown to Western audiences.

These things, combined with the general lack of knowledge in the West about Eastern Christianity in the West, make it easy for Western media and individuals to ignore this debate and consequently the significant religious dimension at the heart, not only of the conflict in Ukraine, but of Russian aggression writ large (not to mention the significant role of contemporary Eastern Christianity in other geopolitical hotspots like Syria, Turkey and Cyprus). The erasure of the Eastern Christian presence in these situations in Western media and discourse clouds our understanding of significant parts of the global picture and renders flat a complex and multidimensional picture.

However, much worse than the erasure of Eastern Christianity and its culture is its complete conflation with Western Christianity, either by failing to acknowledge differences at all or by only highlighting Eastern Christianity through the stories of its

Western converts. (Think about why it is a problem that Richard Gere is probably the most famous Buddhist you can name outside of the Dalai Lama; not to mention the fact that, in the case of Orthodoxy, this often results in non-Western convert communities, such as in sub-Saharan Africa and South Korea, being completely ignored.) This conflation ignores the very real history of conquest and occupation that occurred between Western and Eastern Christendom, in which the West has almost always been the aggressor, that stands as one of the foundations of modern Eastern Christian identity.

For example, the 1204 Sack of Constantinople by Crusaders, so pivotal in Orthodox Christian self-understanding, is virtually unknown in the West. Yet it underlies Patriarch Kirill's defence of Russian aggression in Ukraine, even when it sounds to Western ears like standard conservative Christian fare. It also stands at the centre of more progressive Orthodox Christian conversations, for example around colonialism as a paradigm for talking about the Eastern Christian experience. (Google the history of the Ukrainian Greek Catholic Church – it might surprise you.)

Conflation with Western Christianity also silences the ongoing and powerful debates within Eastern Christianity about the West that, as discussed above, are at the heart of so much contemporary geopolitical conflict: if all Christianity is Western in reality or origin, why would any Christian group need to negotiate its relationship with the West? If the conflicts within Eastern Christianity are only heard in the voices and experiences of its Western converts (voices and experiences free from the specific historical and generational trauma that pervades so many Eastern Christian cultures), why are its debates any different from those in the West?

In fact, Eastern Christianity (and the culture it arises from and produces) is unique – as distinct in many ways as Islamic or

Confucian civilization is from the West. It has its own history, memory, values and customs, all of which are distinct from its Western counterpart, despite a common source.

You may never have heard of Russia World or the Kyivan Rus or Holy Russia before this war began. It is possible you still only vaguely know what the Byzantine Empire was. That is okay. For now. But arguably the top six most religious countries in Europe are all Eastern Christian nations by heritage and identity. Inarguably, there are more Orthodox Christians in the USA than Unitarians. This is not a fringe category. And as recent events in Russia highlight, Eastern Christianity, and its distinctiveness, can no longer be ignored.

March 24, 2022

Holy Father you are not helping: the problem with the Pope's plan to consecrate Russia and Ukraine to the Immaculate Heart of Mary

The Feast of the Annunciation falls on 25 March, it is the celebration of the day that the Angel Gabriel is said to have appeared to the Virgin Mary to announce that she would bear Christ. It is a date of great significance to Roman Catholics and Eastern Orthodox Christians, one of the major feasts focused upon the Virgin Mary.

The Vatican has announced that, this year, on the Feast of the Annunciation the Pope will consecrate Russia and Ukraine to the Immaculate Heart of Mary. While it would be unfair to assume bad intentions, it is yet another glaring misstep in the Pontiff's handling of the Russian invasion of Ukraine. It is also a stark, and extremely public, reminder of the West's entirely unhelpful – and historically tone deaf – approach to Orthodox Christianity.

The Pope's decision to carry out the consecration service dates to a series of appearances of the Virgin Mary reported by three shepherd children in the small village of Fatima, Portugal, between the spring of 1916 and the autumn of 1917. During the appearance, the children received a series of prophecies and requests, among them that Russia (then in the midst of the Bolshevik Revolution) would be consecrated to the Immaculate Heart of Mary so that it would be converted.

While it is easy for Western Christians, particularly for Catholics, to see this prophecy and subsequent consecration as a response to the threat of atheist Communism facing Russia at the time of the apparition, it is difficult for Orthodox Christians to not see the prophecy that Russia will be 'converted' in the light of the now nearly thousand years of tension (and sometimes open warfare) between Western and Eastern Christendom, a history that has frequently seen the Catholic Church operate in the role of aggressor or opportunist.

This history begins roughly in 1054, the formal break in communion between the Latin Western Christian Church, headed by the Roman papacy, and the four historical patriarchates of the Eastern Church. The split was preceded by a series of disputes concerning both Church governance and theology, chief among them contention over the Pope's claim to universal authority.

A number of violent incidents over 200 years, from both sides of Christianity's two halves, helped solidify the separation. These included the Byzantine massacre of Catholics living in Constantinople in 1182, the sacking of Thessaloniki by Catholics in 1185 and their pillage of Constantinople in 1204. Finally, the establishment of Rome-allied episcopacies in traditionally Eastern Christian territory captured by Crusaders further cemented the divide.

While the history of Western Christianity since that time has been a history of relative power and prominence, the Eastern Christian world has had a rockier ride, from Ottoman occupation to Soviet repression. Throughout this period, it is difficult not to notice that the West – the rich, powerful twin – has seldom missed an opportunity to leverage Eastern Christian misfortune to its own advantage. The Crusades themselves are a prime example, but Catholic power grabs in places like Ukraine during the sixteenth century around the fall of Constantinople also illustrate this problem.

Which brings us back to Thursday's consecration. The doctrine of the Immaculate Conception, which holds that the Virgin Mary was free from Original Sin, is not a doctrine shared between the Catholic and Orthodox Churches. In fact, it has only been an official part of Catholic teaching since 1854. While the Eastern Churches agree with Catholics that Mary was free from personal sin, the fact that the Eastern Church has never accepted Augustine's teaching on Original Sin means that the doctrine is superfluous for Eastern Christian theology.

The Doctrine of the Immaculate Conception is also one of the most hotly contested theological issues in ecumenical dialogue between East and West, right up there with papal primacy and the filioque (the 'and the son' part of the Nicene Creed) – two issues that helped drive the split in the first place.

In light of this history, consecrating two countries with overwhelmingly Orthodox majorities to the Immaculate Heart of Mary, particularly in response to a prophecy that one of those countries will be converted, is, at best, problematic. On an entirely pragmatic level, these kinds of actions feed the fears of the most reactionary elements in the Orthodox world, for whom the fear of Western encroachment is very real. As these are the forces that we are all collectively interested in keeping at bay, adding fuel to their fire seems ill advised.

Also, it is really not okay to make other people your non-consensual missionary project. And it is nonsensical to try to convert a person – or a country – that is already converted. Unless you do not think they really are converted; and as we have already discussed, in light of the history of East–West Christian relations, it is easy to see this ritual as implying exactly that.

On top of all that we have to ask just how helpful it is to be consecrating Ukraine and Russia at the same time, because of a prophecy about Russia, when the two countries are engaged in a war in which the independence of Ukraine is at issue.

To be clear, there is almost certainly no ill intent on the part of Pope Francis, the Vatican or the many well-meaning Catholics cheering this on. They all probably believe they are doing a very good thing. However, that is the problem of making other people – particularly other people with whom your people already have a tense history – your project. Also, it is genuinely a good idea to check with people before you try to help, whether materially or metaphysically. Sometimes people do not need your kind of help.

Why didn't the Vatican suggest special papal-led prayers to the Virgin Mary for Russia and Ukraine, perhaps including the Eastern Christian bishops resident in Rome? That could be worked out, in theory. Marian devotion is shared between the two ancient halves of the Christian world. Why include so explicitly a doctrine that can be seen as a symbol of Catholic attempts to change Orthodox theology? It is simply tone deaf and insensitive to the wounds of history.

So (and I genuinely cannot believe I am writing this), Pope Francis: Russia and Ukraine are #NotYourMissionField. Please try to find another way to help.

April 8, 2022

Another important defection from the Russian Patriarchate looms; the fate of Orthodoxy in the West hangs in the balance

As the rhetoric of the Russian Orthodox Church grew even more shocking and dangerous this week, an anonymous group of students at the famed St Sergius Orthodox Theological Institute in Paris have sent a letter asking their local bishop, Metropolitan John (Reneto), to leave the Moscow Patriarchate – led by Putin crony Kirill – for the ecclesiastical jurisdiction of Constantinople which opposes the war.

The Institute is in a similar political and cultural situation to St Nicholas in Amsterdam, the famed Russian Orthodox parish that broke away from Moscow last month after its pleas to Patriarch Kirill to call for an end to the violence in Ukraine were met with retaliation, both online and in real life. It is worth noting that St Sergius has only recently become part of the Moscow Patriarchate. For most of its history it was under Constantinople, until 2018, when it was handed over to Moscow as a (clearly unaccepted) consolation prize for an independent Church in Ukraine. This is important, because it does beg the question of whether or not St Sergius would have in fact ever been as vibrant and important an intellectual centre if it had spent its whole life under Moscow.

Founded in 1925, St Sergius is the oldest Orthodox theological school in the West and holds a unique and storied place in the history not only of twentieth-century Orthodox academic theology, but of Orthodox Christianity's larger engagement with Western modernity. The Institute is the child of the post-Revolution Russian emigré community in Paris and has been the intellectual home of some of Orthodoxy's most important and (if the term has meaning in this deeply conservative and tradition-bound world) modern thinkers, among them Father Alexander Schmemann, who was both a student and teacher at the Institute.

In 1951, Father Schmemann came to the USA to teach at St Vladimir's Theological Seminary. The seminary (known as St Vlad's to virtually everyone), like St Sergius, was founded by refugees from the Bolsheviks and is the second oldest Orthodox seminary in the USA, second only to the Greek Orthodox-run Holy Cross Theological School which began the year before. While St Vlad's was already in its second decade by the time Father Schmemann arrived, it is not incorrect to think of it as 'the house that Father Schmemann built'.

He became Dean in 1962, a post he held until his death in 1983. During the 21 years of his deanship, Father Schemmann published some of the most important Orthodox theological treatises ever written in English. Among them was the highly influential *For the Life of the World*, a reflection on liturgical worship and Christian faith.

As an adjunct professor at a number of non-Orthodox seminaries, as well as one of the first preeminent Orthodox theologians to write and publish primarily in English, Father Schmemann was critical in introducing Orthodoxy to America – and, importantly, in introducing America to Orthodoxy.

Father Schmemann's life and theological work are a testament to an open kind of Orthodox Christian theology and faith, the very kind of expression of Orthodoxy that is being challenged (and one could say, intentionally dismantled) by Kirill and his allies. If Father Schmemann's deanship at St Vladimir represented the possibility of Orthodox Christianity enjoying a thriving and intellectually robust life in the modern age, the patriarchate of Kirill represents the renunciation of that possibility.

This is because, today, Father Schmemann's legacy at St Vlad's is under serious threat, and his legacy can be viewed as a bellwether of American Orthodox Christianity. The seminary has come to be dominated by ultra-conservative American converts from various Protestant denominations, largely part of the wave of Protestant conservative Culture Warriors into the Orthodox Church that began in the 1980s. They have mostly succeeded in turning the school into a fortress in their on-going battle against the forces of modernity.

When the school is not hosting ecumenical dialogue between the Orthodox Church in America (the Orthodox jurisdiction that oversees it) and the conservative breakaway Anglican Church in North America, it is hosting Metropolitan Hilarion (Alfeyev), the ultra-conservation Russian Orthodox bishop who has his eyes on being the next Patriarch of Moscow, and a man who once said that women who are victims of domestic violence should not discuss their abuse in public because, 'discussing these issues one way or another is propaganda for sin'. (Importantly, St Vladimir's invitation came two years after these remarks.)

Notably Metropolitan Hilarion has, since the Russian invasion of Ukraine, been stripped of his professorship at the University of Fribourg in Switzerland, although St Vlad's has not returned the $250,000 it received from an anonymous donor to establish The Patriarch Kirill of Moscow and all Rus' Endowment for Biblical Studies, right around the time of Metropolitan Hilarion's lecture last year.

Which brings us back to St Sergius. When the seminary was transferred to the Moscow Patriarchate from Constantinople, there was some suggestion that it would be left alone, merely to be used by Kirill and his allies against charges that they were totalitarian reactionaries, a token jewel of free thought in the tsar-like crown of Moscow. And this has, for the most part, been true. But, like so many tenuous situations in the Orthodox Christian world, the Russian invasion of Ukraine has rendered this situation no longer tenable.

Orthodox Christian seminaries and theological schools are a relatively recent and still quite rare phenomenon in the West. As such, they serve as important locations for dialogue between the West and the Orthodox Christian world. Guarding their moral and intellectual integrity should be of utmost concern. There is an argument to be made that St Vladimir's Seminary has already been lost in this battle. If St Sergius is lost, the hope for a healthy, pluralist, democratic Orthodox Christianity, in America and beyond – one that acts as a counterweight to the authoritarian strain preferred by the Moscow Patriarchate – will take another blow. And that is an outcome that should not be allowed to come to pass.

April 14, 2022

Be careful what you wish for. The downside of kicking the Russian Orthodox Church out of the World Council of Churches

Calls have grown for the Russian Orthodox Church to be expelled from the World Council of Churches (WCC) as a response to the support of the Moscow-based, Patriarch Kirill-led Church for the Russian invasion of Ukraine. This effort has in recent days garnered some prominent supporters, including the former Archbishop of Canterbury, Rowan Williams.

While it is, in light of recent events, clearly no longer sustainable for the Russian Orthodox Church to continue as part of the WCC, it is also worth noting that the exclusion of the Russian Church undoubtedly will have some negative unintended consequences. To begin with, one must consider the current intra-Orthodox conflict in which those within the Orthodox world who wish to reconcile their faith with modern liberalism and the wider world are pitted against those who have adopted a much more reactionary posture, rejecting not only modern liberalism but also what this faction views as hostile outsiders, such as 'the West'.

Furthermore, there is Orthodoxy's rather rocky history with the WCC, a history that emerges from this same conflict. And it is not unreasonable to fear that such a move by the WCC will only stand to empower Patriarch Kirill and the regressive elements within the Orthodox Christian world.

Orthodox Christianity's history with the WCC is in many ways reflective of that intra-Orthodox conflict that is now seemingly at fever pitch, but which has been brewing for the better part of the modern era. In this ongoing debate, ecumenism (the idea that Christians across denominational lines should work towards unity) has been a significant point of contention. The modern ecumenical movement is largely understood to have begun in the late nineteenth or early twentieth century (depending, not surprisingly, on where your denominational sympathies lie).

Regardless, the Orthodox Christian involvement in modern ecumenism undoubtedly began in 1920, when the then-Ecumenical Patriarchate of Constantinople, Germanus V, issued an encyclical letter to 'all the Churches of Christ' in which he encouraged the creation of an organized body of Christian Churches in order to promote trust and co-operation among Christianity's fractured parts.

The Ecumenical Patriarchate would go on to be a founding member of the WCC. There has been a permanent representative from the Ecumenical Patriarchate at the WCC since 1955, while the Russian Orthodox Church has had a permanent representative since 1962. The current acting secretary of the WCC is Revd Prof. Dr Ioan Sauca, a Romanian Orthodox priest, whose own Church has often found itself caught in the crossfire between the two competing Orthodox camps, but has, since the invasion of Ukraine, adopted a much more stridently anti-Russian stance. Although many do not believe he has gone far enough and accusations remain that he is 'soft on Russia'.

However, despite all of this, Orthodox participation in the ecumenical movement generally, and in the WCC specifically, has been far from a straightforward, or a purely positive affair. While ecumenical co-operation was never universally popular among the Orthodoxy, beginning in the 1990s, conservative forces within Orthodoxy began to push for more visibility against Orthodox participation in the ecumenical movement, specifically against participation in the WCC. Some of this opposition was connected to ecclesiological beliefs and an effort to assert Orthodox self-understanding as the 'one True Church'. They feared that ecumenism, in other words, amounted to tacit acceptance of the legitimacy of other ways of being Christian.

For example, the controversial and extremely reactionary Greek Orthodox priest, Father Theodoros Zisis, has written: 'Ecumenism confounds everything. It does not believe that there is Orthodoxy; that there is Truth for which the Saints and Fathers struggled from the time of the Apostles.' Furthermore, many feared that participation in the WCC specifically suggested agreement with the decisions of other members of the council as they liberalized their views on gender and sexuality.

Ultimately, two Orthodox jurisdictions, the Georgian Orthodox Church and the Bulgarian Orthodox Church, left the WCC in the late 1990s. Anti-ecumenist sentiment remains an important pillar of reactionary Orthodox Christian thought with charges of 'ecumenism' regularly invoked alongside accusations of 'innovation' against their more progressive brothers and sisters to undermine the latter's commitment to the Orthodox faith. There remain plenty of Orthodox Christians, both clergy and laity, for whom the WCC symbolizes everything they fear about modernity, progress and the West.

It is this reality that complicates calls to exclude the Russian Orthodox Church from the WCC.

For his part, Patriarch Kirill has been willing to use the WCC and the Russian Orthodox Church's participation within it insofar as it benefits him. In his response to the WCC's call that he condemn violence in Ukraine, Kirill invoked the Toronto Statement, one of the WCC's foundational documents, which notes that the WCC cannot become 'the instrument of one [school]'.

And there is little doubt that Kirill is using both his association with the WCC and his ongoing dialogue with the Vatican as a means by which to assert his ever-waning legitimacy.

However, there is no reason to suggest that there is anything more than pragmatism and expediency at work here. There is nothing in Kirill's words or actions that indicates any genuine commitment to ecumenical dialogue. In fact, one could argue that his behaviour, even towards other Orthodox bishops, suggests that he is completely uninterested in pursuing Christian unity, particularly if that unity comes at the expense of Russian state power.

Any effort to expel the Russian Orthodox Church from the WCC is thus a dangerous one. The expulsion of the Russian Orthodox Church could easily be weaponized by Kirill and Putin to further their position that Russia and the Orthodox Church are under attack from a hostile, decadent West, colluding with sympathetic Orthodox Christians who they imagine seek to destroy Russia, Orthodoxy and the 'traditional' values they promote and defend.

In short, expelling the Russian Orthodox Church from the WCC could very well be used by Kirill as evidence that he has been right about the 'metaphysical battle' that the invasion of Ukraine has represented all along.

Which leaves the WCC with no good options. On the one hand, allowing the Russian Orthodox Church to remain does offer Kirill and his allies legitimacy and cover in their inexcusable actions. On the other, exclusion simply fits the narrative being put forward, not only by Kirill and the Russian Church, but also by reactionary Orthodox Christians across jurisdictions, all too well.

This could very well push ultra-conservative non-Russian Orthodox Christians closer to Moscow even as it provides ammunition to use against other, more liberally minded

Orthodox Christians, creating in reality the false choice between ecumenical dialogue (and by extension engagement with the West and modernity writ large) and Orthodox unity that ultra-conservatives have always said existed.

Calls for Russia to be expelled from the WCC are being made from many corners. Such a reaction is understandable, but let us not pretend that it would come without consequences.

April 22, 2022

Sanctioning Patriarch Kirill would send a strong message

Since the beginning of the Russian invasion of Ukraine, sanctions against Russian officials have been the most visible and powerful form of support offered by the global community to the Ukrainian people. These sanctions have targeted high-ranking Russian officials, oligarchs and their families. Also, since nearly the beginning, when it became increasingly clear that the head of the Russian Orthodox Church, Patriarch Kirill of Moscow, was going to act as a mouthpiece for the Putin regime, there have been isolated calls to sanction the Patriarch and other leading Russian Church officials.

These calls have run parallel to calls to expel the Russian Orthodox Church (ROC) from the World Council of Churches. And while this should probably happen, it is a course of action that will almost inevitably provide some kind of propaganda cover for the ROC as they play along with Kirill's position that he is engaged in some sort of Holy War with the West, one in which he imagines himself as 'the Suffering Servant', excluded by fellow Christians who have lost the True Faith.

But sanctioning Kirill and his coconspirators might actually have a greater effect.

Economic and political sanctions make clear that the problem with Kirill is not primarily his theology, but his politics. The threat that Patriarch Kirill poses to the West is not because he seeks to baptize the secular order, as he would have you believe.

He is a threat because he has allowed the Russian Church to become completely co-opted by the Kremlin.

It is not completely unheard of for religious leaders to be sanctioned when they are complicit in the sorts of things that get laypeople sanctioned. The Supreme Leader of Iran, Ayatollah Khamenei, is currently under sanctions by the USA, as is the Jamaican-based Islamic cleric Abdullah Ibrahim al-Faisal.

That being said, the imposition of sanctions against Christian clerics is far less common, if not entirely non-existent. The USA never placed sanctions on priests who co-operated with the various military dictatorships in Latin America or in Greece (if we are looking for an Orthodox example). Even clerics who co-operated with the apartheid regime in South Africa, arguably one of the most sanctioned governments ever, did not incur any personal penalties.

This discrepancy seems to suggest a part of the problem in the largely Christian West's response to the Russian Orthodox Church: Christian churches and clerics are given greater leeway than Muslim clerics when it comes to supporting dangerous regimes and causes. There is little doubt that if Patriarch Kirill were an ayatollah or a mullah there would be much less question about whether he should be held personally responsible for his complicity in an illegal and increasingly brutal war.

It is also likely that there would be far greater public outcry for his moderate coreligionists to speak out against him – something always demanded of Muslims in analogous situations. Fortunately, even without public pressure, Orthodox Christians who know that Patriarch Kirill cannot speak alone for their tradition are coming forward.

This includes the authors and signatories of the 'Declaration on the "Russian world" (*Russkiy mir*) Teaching', a condemnation of the core ideological and theological propositions being put forward by Kirill and his cronies. There are the parishes in

Western Europe refusing to commemorate Kirill and breaking with Moscow. And, most importantly, the brave priests within Russia speaking out against their chief bishop's proclamations. These dissenters and others like them represent 'the other side' of the internal conflict within Orthodox Christianity.

And it is not just scholars and clerics; there are also ordinary laypeople, many of whom have largely sat out Orthodoxy's recent ideological battles, who are now feeling compelled to act.

Nadya Bodansky, a Russian-born lawyer, came to the USA 30 years ago. She describes herself as 'an ordinary Orthodoxy Christian appalled by the actions of the Russian Orthodox Church'. Concerned by the lack of public discourse about sanctioning Kirill and senior Russian clerics, she started a Change.org petition calling for these sanctions. Bodansky comments:

> Unfortunately I don't have a good platform that would allow me to reach a wide audience with this, so I am afraid it will just remain a symbolic gesture on my part . . . at least I will know that I did what I could.

Sanctions against clerics are usually largely symbolic gestures. It is highly unlikely that either the Supreme Leader of Iran or the Patriarch of Moscow had plans to turn up at Disneyland this summer. But that is beside the point, because symbols matter. Sanctioning Patriarch Kirill and his fellow clerical enablers of Vladimir Putin would be a powerful symbol. One that ought to be deployed.

Conclusion

For most of my life, Orthodoxy felt unquestionably like something that belonged to me and, more importantly, to which I belonged. It was from this deep sense of belonging that I began to write and speak publicly about Orthodox Christianity outside of academic settings, seeking to explain this often alien and confusing tradition to the unfamiliar or misapprehending. Moreover, I was admittedly horrified as I watched the public face of Orthodoxy become more and more reactionary since the start of the twenty-first century. I felt a duty to offer another, alternative voice. I wanted desperately to speak for the tradition I loved and that had, in its own complex way, loved me. Armed with a belief that my training as a classicist and historian would serve to make my responses neutral and helpful as opposed to apologetic and emotional, I set about my self-appointed task with what I now see was a bit of evangelical zeal. I cannot say with any assurance that I have successfully accomplished anything I set out to do. But a lack of effectiveness has never been enough to shut up this very chatty Greek American woman. Besides, who could miss an opportunity to take part in a moment that is critical for one's fundamental ancestral community?

As has become increasingly clear, the Orthodox Church is in a moment of deep division and, one might even argue, existential crisis. In some ways, this is not unlike the rest of the Christian world, but, as always, Orthodoxy forges its path in its own unique way. Thus, for many outside the insular bubble of the Orthodox world, the divisions that cut deep across it did not seem evident until Russian tanks were well on their way to

Kyiv. But the fissures did not begin with the Russian invasion of Ukraine, the invasion merely made them apparent, and suddenly more relevant, to the wider world. After nearly 500 years, Orthodoxy's failure to reconcile in any meaningful way with modernity, to even engage with the immense chasm that separates 1453 from today, has resulted in nothing short of chaos. For far too long, modern Orthodox Christian identity and culture, born in the midst of a literal siege, has been dominated by a bunker mentality, one in which any change is met with suspicion if not reflexive resistance. Certainly, 70 years of Communism, largely in traditionally Orthodox lands, has not helped, only serving to further assure the faithful that any concession to the present is a road that leads to wickedness, godlessness and the end of faith. To be this fearful is to be easily exploited, and the fears of the Orthodox faithful have been exploited, by American Evangelicals, like Franklin Graham, and by cynical political actors within traditionally Orthodox Christian countries, not least of whom is Vladimir Putin himself.

Two modern Russian saints

However, there is more to Orthodoxy than the fear and suspicion that has been allowed to fester across the centuries, and I believe that within the tradition is everything that is needed to save it from itself. This confidence is epitomized in my mind by the lives and teachings of two twentieth-century Russian Orthodox women who are now formally commemorated as saints: St Elizabeth, the Grand Duchess and New Martyr of Russia, and St Maria of Paris. In their lives we see an alternative Orthodox (and Russian!) engagement with modernity. And while it breaks my rule against being confessional in any way while writing for a non-Orthodox audience, I think a little hagiography might go a long way here.

In 1864, the woman who would become St Elizabeth was born Her Grand Ducal Highness Princess Elizabeth Alexandra Luise Alice of Hesse and by Rhine. Orphaned by the time she was a teenager, the young princess was brought up in part by her maternal grandmother, Queen Victoria. In 1884, at the age of 20, she was sent to Russia to marry Grand Duke Sergei, the seventh child of Tsar Alexander II. Contrary to popular belief, the foreign brides of Russian royals were not forced to convert to Orthodoxy by law, and it is clear from contemporary accounts, including the Grand Duchess's own letters, that her conversion was freely chosen, noting that it would be 'lying to God to remain outwardly Protestant'.

Her conversion was part of her more general falling in love with Russian culture and the Russian people. And she was instrumental in arranging the marriage of her younger sister Alix to the then Tsarevich, Nicholas, by encouraging a reluctant Alix to embrace Orthodoxy. She loved Russia and Russia loved her.

Her husband, however, was a different matter. It is, of course, impossible to know what occurs in any marriage, let alone a royal marriage from a century ago, but it feels safe to say that Sergei and Elizabeth's marriage was not a happy one. Although most of the immediate records of their marriage, including the couple's letters to one another, have been lost or destroyed, other contemporary accounts do survive. Many of these suggest that Sergei engaged in a succession of affairs with handsome young military officers, while Elizabeth despaired over her failure to become a mother, a failure that some suggest was the result of her husband being unwilling to share her bed.

Whatever the state of their marriage, Segei's assassination by the socialist revolutionary Ivan Kalyayev on 17 February 1905 came as a profound shock that left the Grand Duchess bereft. On the eve of her husband's funeral, having spent the entire day praying in her private chapel, she asked to be taken to the prison where Kalyayev was being held. There played out a scene that has been recounted many times by biographers, hagiographers and disbelieving commentators.

Elizabeth asked the man before her why he had killed her husband. Kalyayev answered coldly: 'I killed Sergei Alexandrovich because he was a weapon of tyranny. I was taking revenge for the people.' Having heard his answer, Elizabeth replied that the man should repent and that she had already forgiven him. As further proof that this forgiveness was genuine, she had inscribed on her husband's tombstone Christ's last words on the Cross: 'Father, forgive them. They know not what they do.' In his biography of Tsar Nicholas II, creatively titled *The Last Tsar,* the Russian writer Edvard Radzinsky says of Elizabeth's reaction to her husband's murder:

> On the eve of revolution, she had already found a way out; forgiveness! Forgive through the impossible pain and blood – and thereby stop it then, at the beginning, this bloody wheel. By her example, poor Ella appealed to society, calling upon the people to live in Christian faith.

Within four years of her husband's death, Elizabeth sold her extensive, priceless collection of clothes and jewels, including her wedding ring. With the proceeds, she founded the Convent of Saints Martha and Mary and became its abbess. In the grounds of the convent, she built a hospital, chapel, pharmacy and orphanage. As the First World War began and the spirit of revolution spread through the streets of Moscow, the abbess, now Mother Elizabeth, and her nuns dedicated themselves to caring for the poor, to nursing the wounds of soldiers and feeding the growing cadre of orphans. The princess nun and her convent were popular in Moscow, which might explain why, in 1918, following the Bolshevik Revolution, Lenin quickly had her arrested.

After her arrest, she was sent further and further east, eventually arriving in Alapayevsk, where she was imprisoned in the Napolnaya School with other members of the royal family. They spent about three months at the school, until, on 17 July 1918, the prisoners were taken away, eventually ending up in a field of iron mines outside the village of Siniachikha. There they were beaten and then thrown alive into the mine shafts. A pious tradition holds that a passer-by heard the Duchess sing the Paschal hymn, 'Christ is Risen', as she lay in the mine waiting to die.

The year before the Grand Duke Sergei was appointed Governor-General of Moscow, in the years in which Elizabeth was fully immersed in the life of a royal princess, a girl was born to an aristocratic family in Riga, then a part of the Russian Empire (now the capital of Latvia), and given the name Elizaveta Pilenko. Her beloved father died while she was a teenager. The sadness and emptiness of the loss convinced the young girl that there could not possibly be a God. Arriving in St Petersburg with her mother at the age of 15, she immediately became involved in radical intellectual circles. By the time she was 19 she had married the Bolshevik Dimitri Kuzmin-Karaviev.

It was a short-lived affair. By 1913, only three years after it had begun, the marriage was over.

With a daughter, Gaiana, now in tow, Elizabeth moved to southern Russia, where, drawn to the humanity of Christ, she began to experience a sense of religious devotion for the first time in her life. But even as her faith began to take root, her radical politics stayed intact. In the aftermath of the 1918 Bolshevik Revolution, she was elected deputy mayor of the town of Anapa and, when the mayor fled in the face of an advancing White Army, she became mayor. When the White Army took the city, Elizabeth was put on trial for being a Bolshevik. Her fate seemed sealed. But, in a coincidence that would be more at home in a Russian novel than real life, the judge was her former teacher,

Daniil Skobtsov. Elizabeth was acquitted. Shortly after, she fell in love with the judge and then married him. (Eat your heart out, Tolstoy. You could never have thought of something that good.)

But there was to be no happy ending. Soon, the new bride (pregnant with her second child) and her husband, along with her mother, were forced to flee an increasingly unstable and unpredictable Russia. They first went to Georgia, where a son, Yuri, was born. Then to Yugoslavia, where she had a daughter, Anastasia. Eventually, in 1923, they ended up in Paris, joining a growing number of Russian refugees in the city.

In Paris, the religious urges that had begun a decade before began to bear fruit. Elizabeth dedicated herself to theological study and social work. In 1926, after having been in Paris only three years, the younger of her daughters died of influenza. Her elder daughter was sent to boarding school in Belgium. Her marriage was falling apart. Her bishop suggested that perhaps she should take monastic vows. She agreed only on the condition that she be allowed to continue to live in the world, not secluded in some remote monastery (the usual fate of women Orthodox monastics).

In 1932, her divorce from Daniil granted, she took her vows, adopting the name 'Maria'. She rented a house in Paris that served as a convent, refuge and salon. She remained an imposing and striking figure. Metropolitan Antony Bloom, who would eventually become the Russian Orthodox Bishop of London, was a young Parisian layman when he met the unconventional nun. Describing their first meeting he said:

> She was a very unusual nun in her behaviour and her manners. I was simply staggered when I saw her for the first time in monastic clothes. I was walking along the Boulevard Montparnasse and I saw: in front of a café, on the pavement, there was a table, on the table was a glass of beer and behind

> the glass was sitting a Russian nun in full monastic robes. I looked at her and decided that I would never go near that woman. I was young then and held extreme views.

In 1940, when Nazi tanks filled the streets of Paris, the house became a known dispensary of false baptismal certificates. Soon the occupying Germans caught on and Mother Maria and her companions were arrested. She was sent to Ravensbruck Concentration Camp where she died in a gas chamber on Holy Saturday, 1945.

I knew none of this when, as a college student, I first encountered St Maria. Such was the distinctly Hellenic character of my Orthodox upbringing, I had heard little of the modern martyrs of the Russian tradition (though I do have a vague recollection of a great-aunt, who was also a strident monarchist, mentioning that the last Tsar and his entire family were 'passion bearers', a kind of accidental martyr). I first met St Maria through her plethora of theological writing. I can still see the sun breaking through the perpetual fog of the San Francisco Bay as I read:

> We cannot see the Church as a sort of aesthetic perfection and limit ourselves to aesthetics swooning — our God-given freedom calls us to activity and struggle. And it would be a great lie to tell searching souls: 'Go to church, because there you will find peace.' The opposite is true. She tells those who are at peace and asleep: 'Go to church, because there you will feel real alarm about your sins, about your perdition, about the world's sins and perdition. There you will feel an unappeasable hunger for Christ's truth. There instead of lukewarm you will become ardent, instead of pacified you will become alarmed, instead of learning the wisdom of this world you will become foolish in Christ.
> Mother Maria Skobtsova, *Essential Writings*, p. 115

I wrote the following words on a notecard, keeping them pinned to the corkboard over my desk, well into my postgraduate years:

> The way to God lies through love of people. At the Last Judgment I shall not be asked whether I was successful in my ascetic exercises, nor how many bows and prostrations I made. Instead I shall be asked did I feed the hungry, clothe the naked, visit the sick and the prisoners. That is all I shall be asked. About every poor, hungry and imprisoned person the Savior says 'I': 'I was hungry and thirsty, I was sick and in prison.' To think that he puts an equal sign between himself and anyone in need. . . . I always knew it, but now it has somehow penetrated to my sinews. It fills me with awe.

And I decided that I might just be able to remain a Christian when I lay on the bed in my cramped apartment on Hearst Ave, directly opposite the UC Berkeley campus and saw the words:

> Christ, who approached prostitutes, tax collectors and sinners, can hardly be the teacher of those who are afraid to soil their pristine garments, who are completely devoted to the letter, who live only by the rules, and who govern their whole life according to rules.
> Mother Maria Skobtsova, *Essential Writings*, p. 154

This was Orthodoxy as I had never experienced it before. And it was while looking for a biography of St Maria that I found St Elizabeth. Another woman defying the norms, or what I imagined were the norms, of my faith. Orthodoxy that, at least at the time, seemed to me to be unencumbered by the heavy weights of tribe and history that had characterized, if not defined, my childhood religion. I realize now that this was an illusion too. It is not as if these two women, no matter how admirable they may have been, managed to escape from everything and emerge in a place where only faith remains. That is not, I have come to believe, something any of us can do, not this side of paradise. But I have been thinking a great deal about both of them since Russia invaded Ukraine over a year ago.

So much of what has been written about the religious dimensions of the war in Ukraine, so much of what I have written, intentionally or not, seems to suggest that there is no other way it could have been – that all of this was ultimately inevitable. I do not, at least on my better days, believe this. I do not believe it because I do not believe that there is one singular Orthodox Christianity and thus I do not believe there is only one possible outcome for the Orthodox world. One of the benefits of an ancient, continuous tradition is that it cannot be homogenous. Too many voices have joined the chorus for all of them to harmonize. Rather than conformity, such a tradition inevitably produces diversity. Certainly, at different times and in different places, some voices will be louder, more present. There will be times when some voices are silent, but all the voices are there ready to emerge again when we are ready to listen. If the Orthodox Church is to survive, and if I can be so bold as to say it, if Christianity is to survive, we must begin by digging back into our traditions and allowing forgotten voices to sing. We need to find other ways to be Orthodox, to be Catholic, to be Anglican or Protestant. Much of the future will be determined by how quickly we can recognize our task and accomplish it. Despite the fatalism I know I inherited from my Orthodox upbring, I am strangely hopeful that we will ultimately succeed in this. At least eventually.

All that being said, I have no more idea than anyone else what will happen in Ukraine and Russia in the months and years ahead. Clearly, the current state of affairs is unsustainable, and how much longer Vladimir Putin and Patriarch Kirill can maintain their tenuous grasp on power remains to be seen. At the very least, we can take comfort in the fact that neither of them is immortal. That is not to say that those waiting in the wings to replace them will be any better. And the historical and cultural circumstances that have allowed them their power remain largely intact. It seems unlikely that peace, at least a lasting and real peace, will come any time soon.

Epilogue

I was baptized when I was six months old at the Assumption Greek Orthodox Cathedral in Glendale, Colorado, feet away from the spot where my parents had been married two years before, feet away from where my grandparents' bodies were laid in flower-lined caskets decades later. Under the giant gold dome of this Byzantine cathedral built by the descendants of Greek immigrant coal miners and ranchers in the heart of the American West, I was brought up in my family's ancient faith.

I cannot remember my baptism, of course, but I have always been able to picture it, because I know the place, the service and actors so well. On that June day, I was made a part of something that I doubt I would have chosen on my own, but that has become dearer to me than anything else. Something that it does not seem possible to me that I could leave, even when I fear it has left me.

I do not like being part of the same religious tradition as Vladimir Putin. I recoil at myself when I reflect upon the fact that I know that I would kiss the hand of Patriarch Kirill were he to stand in front of me, because you kiss the hand of a bishop, even if he is a murderer. My relationship with my religion is far from unambiguous. But my belonging to it is simply a fact, a fact I seem to have no real control over. It is in my DNA. Thus when I think of what should be done, both about my own faith and that of my wider faith community, I think about my grandmother and the way she found to walk the line between tradition and the modern world.

Yiayia Kay kept her scarves in the far upper right-hand corner of the long light oak dresser. By the time I was old enough to remember, she never took them out except to garden. She would drape one of the silk covers over her perfectly coiffed hair to protect it against the dry winds of the Colorado high plains. As a little girl and even into her teens and early married life, these had been more than mere gardening accoutrements. They were the outward visible witness of her inner self, signalling to the world, not just that she was a Christian but that she was a lady, modest and chaste. Then one day, around the time television became king, like so many Greek American women of her generation, she folded up the scarves and put them in the dresser.

The fact is that, for most of my childhood in the urban, assimilated Greek Orthodox parish where I grew up, the head covering was completely absent. The Greek immigrant women of the Mountain West (and elsewhere) had, just two generations before me, an experience not unlike that of Muslim women today with regards to the cultural and religious mandate that they hide their hair. It had made them an object of scorn among their neighbours. It had marked them out not just as different, but backward, laying bare for all to see that the Greeks were not good to their women and that Orthodox Christianity was a tool of oppression, the unenlightened project of the exotic East. It was not until the late 1990s, with an influx of white American converts, that the headscarf appeared in my world. Many of these women did not just wear the scarf in church, they kept their heads covered at all times. They hid their perfect blonde and light brown hair behind silk scarves, headbands and pretty hats. As a teenager who rose an hour early each morning to try and tame my rebellious curls, it amazed me that these women would hide their perfect, shampoo-commercial-approved hair. Frankly, it seemed like such a waste. Yet even as more women came with their head scarves, the Greek grandmothers kept their heads bare – almost defiantly. They would not be dragged back.

When I asked my mother why Yiayia stopped wearing the veil, years after my grandmother was gone, my mother said that for my Yiayia it came down to modesty (even in the face of her other considerations). Modesty as both women had been quick to remind me is 'not a line you draw on your knee. It is a line you draw on your heart.' It means not calling attention to yourself. Not asking the world to view you as the most beautiful or the most holy. When everyone was wearing a headscarf, you wore it. But when you found yourself in a time and place where women had taken it off, you took it off as well. Any other choice was an egregious display of self-aggrandizement.

I think that the Orthodox world might have something to learn from my grandmother's example in its wrestling with modernity. Putting on shows of piety is not the way of real holiness. In fact, as we have seen in Russia over the past year, shows of piety are frequently smoke screens for the most horrific deeds. It is easy to point to events in the history of the Christian East, and of Russia specifically, that have made such displays of piety almost reflexive, but that does not make them right or just or even a very good idea. Much of what will happen next depends upon our collective ability to realize this.

Until that time, I have replaced the St Maria of Paris quote above my desk with another observation by the unusual nun from Paris. Written in early days of the Second World War, her words seem almost prophetic now:

> Such terrible times are coming, the world is so exhausted from its scabs and sores, it so cries out to Christianity in the secret depths of its soul, but at the same time it is so far

removed from Christianity, that Christianity cannot and dare not show it a distorted, diminished, darkened image of itself. It should scorch the world with the flame of Christ's love, it should go to the cross on behalf of the world. It should incarnate Christ Himself in it.
Mother Maria Skobtsova, *Essential Writings*, p. 186

Select bibliography

Ancient sources

The Alexiad

This chronicle of the reign of Alexios I Komenos was written around 1148 by the Emperor's daughter Anne Komena. It provides our best source for an Eastern account of the First Crusade.

Evidences of History

The most important work of the late Byzantine historian Laonikos Chalkokondyles, this text provides a comprehensive account of the last 150 years of the Eastern Empire.

Historia Turco-Byzantine

Preserved not only in Greek, but in an old Italian version, which is more complete than the Greek, this account by the Byzantine historian Michael Doukas begins with the Battle of Kosovo in 1389 until the Ottoman conquest of Lesvos in 1462.

The Primary Chronicle

The most comprehensive and important source for the medieval history of the Eastern Slavs, roughly covering the period between 850 and 1110. It is likely that *The Primary Chronicle* was first compiled at Kyiv around 1113.

Modern works

Victoria Clarke, *Why Angels Fall: A Journey Through Orthodox Europe, from Byzantium to Kosovo*, Palgrave MacMillian, 2000

Orlando Figes, *Natasha's Dance: A Cultural History of Russia,* Picador, 2003

Jonathan Harris *The Lost World of Byzantium*, Yale University Press, 2014

Jonathan Philips, *The Fourth Crusade and the Sack of Constantinople*, Penguin Books, 2005

Father Alexander Schmemann, *For the Life of the World: Sacraments and Orthodoxy*, St Vladimir's Seminary Press, new edition, 2018

Mother Maria Skobtsova, *Essential Writings*, Orbis Books, 2002

Index

Index

Index